endorsed for
edexcel

Edexcel GCSE (9-1)
History

Weimar and Nazi Germany, 1918–39

Series Editor: Angela Leonard

ALWAYS LEARNING **PEARSON**

Published by Pearson Education Limited, 80 Strand, London, WC2R 0RL.

www.pearsonschoolsandfecolleges.co.uk

Copies of official specifications for all Edexcel qualifications may be found on the website: www.edexcel.com

Text © Pearson Education Limited 2016

Series editor: Angela Leonard
Designed by Colin Tilley Loughrey, Pearson Education Limited
Typeset by Phoenix Photosetting, Chatham, Kent
Original illustrations © Pearson Education Limited
Illustrated by KJA Artists Illustration Agency and Phoenix Photosetting, Chatham, Kent.

Cover design by Colin Tilley Loughrey
Picture research by Christine Martin
Cover photo © Front: Bridgeman Art Library Ltd: Private Collection

The right of John Child to be identified as author of this work has been asserted by him in accordance with the Copyright, Designs and Patents Act 1988.

First published 2016
Fifth impression 2018

19 18
10 9 8 7 6 5

British Library Cataloguing in Publication Data
A catalogue record for this book is available from the British Library.
ISBN 978 1 292 12734 7

Printed in China(GCC)

A note from the publisher
In order to ensure that this resource offers high-quality support for the associated Pearson qualification, it has been through a review process by the awarding body. This process confirms that this resource fully covers the teaching and learning content of the specification or part of a specification at which it is aimed. It also confirms that it demonstrates an appropriate balance between the development of subject skills, knowledge and understanding, in addition to preparation for assessment.

Endorsement does not cover any guidance on assessment activities or processes (e.g. practice questions or advice on how to answer assessment questions), included in the resource nor does it prescribe any particular approach to the teaching or delivery of a related course.

While the publishers have made every attempt to ensure that advice on the qualification and its assessment is accurate, the official specification and associated assessment guidance materials are the only authoritative source of information and should always be referred to for definitive guidance.

Pearson examiners have not contributed to any sections in this resource relevant to examination papers for which they have responsibility.

Examiners will not use endorsed resources as a source of material for any assessment set by Pearson.

Endorsement of a resource does not mean that the resource is required to achieve this Pearson qualification, nor does it mean that it is the only suitable material available to support the qualification, and any resource lists produced by the awarding body shall include this and other appropriate resources.

Websites
Pearson Education Limited is not responsible for the content of any external internet sites. It is essential for tutors to preview each website before using it in class so as to ensure that the URL is still accurate, relevant and appropriate. We suggest that tutors bookmark useful websites and consider enabling students to access them through the school/college intranet.

Contents

How to use this book

What's covered?

This book covers the Modern Depth study on Weimar and Nazi Germany, 1918–39. This unit makes up 30% of your GCSE course, and will be examined in Paper 2.

Modern depth studies cover a short period of time, and require you to know about a society or historical situation in detail. You need to understand different aspects within this period, such as social, economic, political, cultural and military, and how they interact with each other. This book also explains the different types of exam questions you will need to answer, and includes advice and example answers to help you improve.

Features

As well as a clear, detailed explanation of the key knowledge you will need, you will also find a number of features in the book:

Key terms

Where you see a word followed by an asterisk, like this: Electorate*, you will be able to find a Key Terms box on that page that explains what the word means.

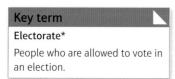

Key term

Electorate*
People who are allowed to vote in an election.

Activities

Every few pages, you'll find a box containing some activities designed to help check and embed knowledge and get you to really think about what you've studied. The activities start simple, but might get more challenging as you work through them.

Summaries and Checkpoints

At the end of each chunk of learning, the main points are summarised in a series of bullet points – great for embedding the core knowledge, and handy for revision.

Checkpoints help you to check and reflect on your learning. The Strengthen section helps you to consolidate knowledge and understanding, and check that you've grasped the basic ideas and skills. The Challenge questions push you to go beyond just understanding the information, and into evaluation and analysis of what you've studied.

Sources and Interpretations

This book contains numerous contemporary pictorial and text sources that show what people from the period, said, thought or created.

The book also includes extracts from the work of historians, showing how experts have interpreted the events you've been studying.

You will need to be comfortable examining both sources AND interpretations to answer questions in your Paper 3 exam.

Source A

A German poster from 1931. It advertises a NSDAP rally and shows a German figure in handcuffs labelled 'Versailles'.

Interpretation 1

From *The Coming of the Third Reich* by Richard J. Evans, published in 2004.

No one was prepared for the peace terms... All of this was greeted with incredulous horror by the majority of Germans. The sense of outrage and disbelief... was almost universal. Germany's international strength and prestige had been on an upward course since unification in 1871... now, suddenly, Germany had been brutally expelled from the ranks of the Great Powers and covered in what they considered to be undeserved shame. Versailles was condemned as a dictated peace, unilaterally imposed without the possibility of negotiation.

Extend your knowledge

These features contain useful additional information that adds depth to your knowledge, and to your answers. The information is closely related to the key issues in the unit, and questions are sometimes included, helping you to link the new details to the main content.

Extend your knowledge

First World War literature
Erich Remarque wrote a gritty, realistic anti-war novel called *All Quiet on the Western Front*. Published in 1929, it sold 500,000 copies in three months and was adapted into a film. How was this book similar to work in other areas of the Arts in Germany in the 1920s?

Exam-style questions and tips

The book also includes extra exam-style questions you can use to practise. These appear in the chapters and are accompanied by a tip to help you get started on an answer.

Exam-style question, Section B

Study Source B (page 28) and Source F (page 31).

How useful are Source B and Source F for an enquiry into the recovery of the Weimar Republic between 1923 and 1929?

Explain your answer, using Source B, Source F and your knowledge of the historical context.   **8 marks**

Exam tip

A good answer will consider:

- how useful the information in each source is for this particular enquiry
- how the provenance (i.e. the type of source, its origin, author or purpose) of each source affects how useful it is
- how knowledge of history at that time affects a judgement of how useful each source is.

Recap pages

At the end of each chapter, you'll find a page designed to help you to consolidate and reflect on the chapter as a whole. Each recap page includes a recall quiz, ideal for quickly checking your knowledge or for revision. Recap pages also include activities designed to help you summarise and analyse what you've learned, and also reflect on how each chapter links to other parts of the unit.

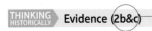
THINKING HISTORICALLY

These activities are designed to help you develop a better understanding of how history is constructed, and are focused on the key areas of Evidence, Interpretations, Cause & Consequence and Change & Continuity. In the Modern Depth Study, you will come across activities on Cause & Consequence, Evidence and Interpretations as these are key areas of focus for this unit.

The Thinking Historically approach has been developed in conjunction with Dr Arthur Chapman and the Institute of Education, UCL. It is based on research into the misconceptions that can hold students back in history.

THINKING HISTORICALLY | Evidence (2b&c) — conceptual map reference

The Thinking Historically conceptual map can be found at: www.pearsonschools.co.uk/thinkinghistoricallygcse

WRITING HISTORICALLY

At the end of most chapters is a spread dedicated to helping you improve your writing skills. These include simple techniques you can use in your writing to make your answers clearer, more precise and better focused on the question you're answering.

The Writing Historically approach is based on the *Grammar for Writing* pedagogy developed by a team at the University of Exeter and popular in many English departments. Each spread uses examples from the preceding chapter, so it's relevant to what you've just been studying.

Preparing for your exams

At the back of the book, you'll find a special section dedicated to explaining and exemplifying the new Edexcel GCSE History exams. Advice on the demands of this paper, written by Angela Leonard, helps you prepare for and approach the exam with confidence. Each question type is explained through annotated sample answers at two levels, showing clearly how answers can be improved.

Pearson Progression Scale: This icon indicates the Step that a sample answer has been graded at on the Pearson Progression Scale.

This book is also available as an online ActiveBook, which can be licensed for your whole institution.

There is also an ActiveLearn Digital Service available to support delivery of this book, featuring a front-of-class version of the book, lesson plans, worksheets, exam practice PowerPoints, assessments, notes on Thinking Historically and Writing Historically, and more.

ActiveLearn
Digital Service

Timeline: Weimar and Nazi Germany, 1918–39

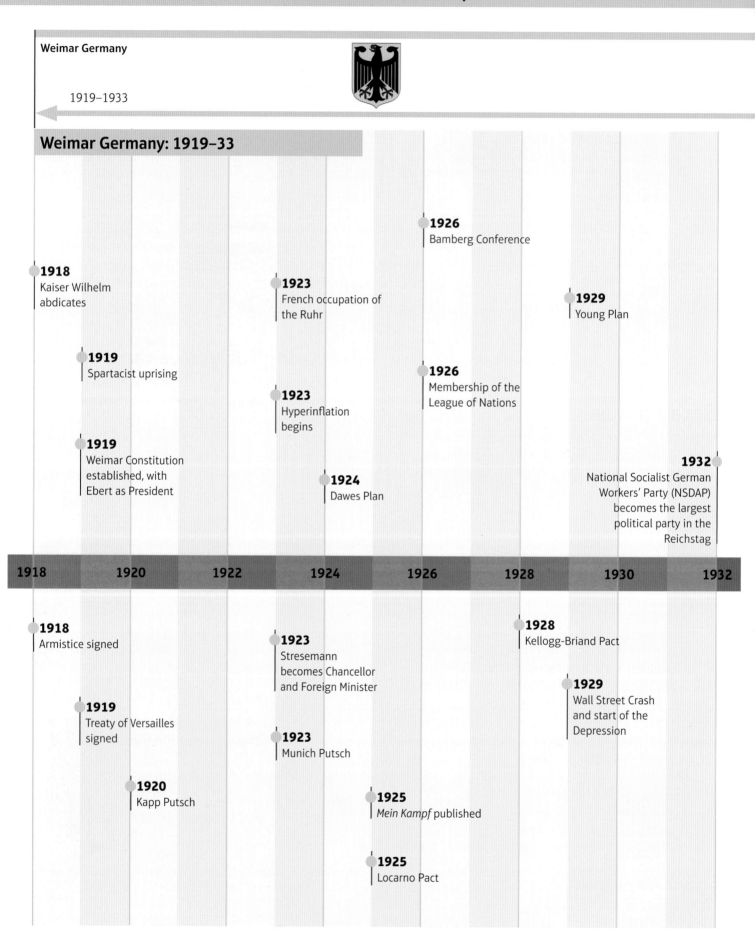

Weimar Germany

1919–1933

Weimar Germany: 1919–33

1926
Bamberg Conference

1918
Kaiser Wilhelm
abdicates

1923
French occupation of
the Ruhr

1929
Young Plan

1919
Spartacist uprising

1926
Membership of the
League of Nations

1923
Hyperinflation
begins

1919
Weimar Constitution
established, with
Ebert as President

1932
National Socialist German
Workers' Party (NSDAP)
becomes the largest
political party in the
Reichstag

1924
Dawes Plan

1918	1920	1922	1924	1926	1928	1930	1932

1918
Armistice signed

1923
Stresemann
becomes Chancellor
and Foreign Minister

1928
Kellogg-Briand Pact

1919
Treaty of Versailles
signed

1929
Wall Street Crash
and start of the
Depression

1923
Munich Putsch

1920
Kapp Putsch

1925
Mein Kampf published

1925
Locarno Pact

Nazi Germany

1933–1939

Nazi Germany: 1933–1945

1933
Hitler appointed as
Chancellor

1933
Reichstag Fire

1935
Nuremberg Laws
passed

1933
Enabling Law passed

1938
Kristallnacht
(Night of
Broken Glass)

1934
Night of the Long
Knives

| 1933 | 1934 | 1935 | 1936 | 1937 | 1938 |

1933
People asked to
boycott Jewish shops

1936
Berlin Olympics

1933
Gestapo (secret
police) established

1933
Concordat with
Catholic Church

1934
Death of Hindenburg
and Hitler becomes
Führer

01 | The Weimar Republic, 1918–29

By November 1918, the First World War had been going on for four years.

The German army was still deadlocked against the armies of the Allies (including Britain, France and the United States). The Allies were gradually gaining the upper hand, but Germany was still undefeated on the battlefield.

However, back at home, the German state was crumbling. Demonstrations, strikes, revolts and mutinies had broken out across the country. Between November 1918 and July 1919, in a series of events known as the German revolution, the Kaiser abdicated and a new German state – the Weimar Republic – was formed.

However, the new Weimar Republic was crippled from the start. It carried wounds inflicted by four years of warfare. It was resented by a large part of the German people. It was also governed under a flawed constitution.

The Weimar Republic had a difficult birth.

Learning outcomes

In this chapter, you will learn about:

- the origins of the Weimar Republic, 1918–19
- the early political and economic challenges to the Republic, 1919–23
- the political and economic recovery of the Republic, 1919–23
- changes in German society, 1924–29.

The legacy of the First World War

During the First World War, Germany had faced the combined might of the Allies, which included Britain, France, Russia, Italy and the USA. It had been a long, bloody and expensive war.

- Fighting had lasted four years, from 1914 to 1918.
- Eleven million Germans fought in the war. Almost two million German troops died and over four million were wounded – so 55% of German troops became casualties.
- The cost of the war meant that the German government's debts trebled between 1914 and 1918, from 50 billion marks to 150 billion marks.

However, it wasn't just German troops and the German government who suffered. The German people suffered too. For example, the British Navy blockaded German ports, preventing German ships bringing food into the country. Over 750,000 Germans died because of food shortages during the First World War.

As a result of this suffering, Germany started to crumble from within before it was ever defeated on the battlefield. The map below gives details of the unrest in Germany by November 1918.

In Berlin, the capital, it was clear that Kaiser Wilhelm (the German emperor) and his ministers had lost control of Germany. It was time for him to go.

Source A

From the papers of Jan Smuts, a South African politician who visited Germany in 1918.

```
... mother-land of our
civilization [Germany] lies
in ruins, exhausted by the
most terrible struggle in
history, with its peoples
broke, starving, despairing,
from sheer nervous
exhaustion, mechanically
struggling forward along the
paths of anarchy [disorder
with no strong authority]
and war.
```

Interpretation 1

From *The Weimar Republic* by John Hiden, published in 1996.

In the face of such pressure, existing order virtually collapsed. The rapid spread throughout Germany of workers' and soldiers' councils confirmed that people were attracted to the prospect of far-reaching political change.

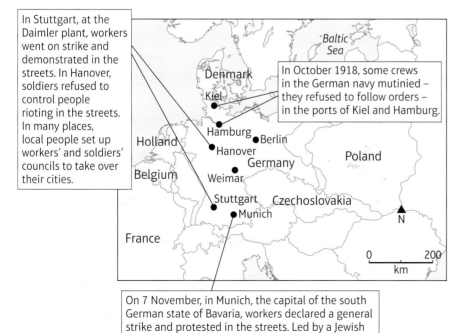

In Stuttgart, at the Daimler plant, workers went on strike and demonstrated in the streets. In Hanover, soldiers refused to control people rioting in the streets. In many places, local people set up workers' and soldiers' councils to take over their cities.

In October 1918, some crews in the German navy mutinied – they refused to follow orders – in the ports of Kiel and Hamburg.

On 7 November, in Munich, the capital of the south German state of Bavaria, workers declared a general strike and protested in the streets. Led by a Jewish communist, named Kurt Eisner, they announced that they were separate from the rest of Germany.

Figure 1.1 A map showing unrest in Germany by November 1918.

The German revolution, 1918–19

By November 1918, the **German revolution** had already begun. As the map on page 9 shows, Kaiser Wilhelm's government had lost control of the country to strikers and rioters. In many towns, workers and soldiers had set up their own, unofficial councils to replace the Kaiser's officials.

The abdication* of the Kaiser

On 9 November 1918, the Kaiser was at the army headquarters in the town of Spa, 700 kilometres from the capital, Berlin. His ministers told him that the only way to restore order in Germany was for him to abdicate, giving up his position as the emperor of Germany. At first, he refused.

However, the Kaiser had lost the support of the German army. The officers at army headquarters refused to support him. When told this news by General Wilhelm Groener, the army's second-in-command, the Kaiser had no choice. On 9 November, he abdicated and, in the early hours of 10 November, went into exile in Holland.

The declaration of a republic

On 9 November, the streets of Berlin were full of people. Some gathered peacefully outside the Reichstag, the German parliament, while others collected guns and took over parts of the city.

Inside the Reichstag was Philipp Scheidemann, a leading member of the Social Democratic Party (SPD), the biggest party in the German parliament. He was told that armed rioters were preparing to announce a communist* government in Berlin. Scheidemann was keen to retain control of events and keep a more moderate form of government. He rushed to an open window of the Reichstag and proclaimed to the crowds below that the Kaiser had gone and that there was a new German Republic. He appealed for a peaceful transition to the new regime (see Source B).

Source B

Scheidemann's appeal from the balcony of the Reichstag on 9 November 1918.

```
The Hohenzollerns [the German royal family]
have abdicated. Take care not to allow
anything to mar this proud day. Long live
the German Republic.
```

The Council of People's Representatives

The SPD had to work quickly to establish the new republic.

- On 9 November, the Kaiser's chancellor (equivalent to a British prime minister), Max von Baden, handed over his office to Friedrich Ebert, the leader of the SPD.
- On 10 November, Ebert made an agreement with General Groener for the army to work with the government to keep the communists out of power.
- Also on 10 November, Ebert suspended the old Reichstag (parliament) and named six moderate politicians who would form the Council of People's Representatives. This council would head the government of the country, but only until a new constitution* could be agreed.
- By taking these steps, moderate politicians in the SPD were able to take control of Germany, preventing anarchy or a takeover by communist extremists.

Key terms

Abdication*

A leader, like a king, queen or emperor, giving up their throne or position.

Communist*

Communism is an extreme form of government, in which representatives of the workers set up a government and take over ownership of all land, property and resources in a country. It was associated with Germany's enemy, Russia.

Constitution*

The rules which set out how a country is run.

The armistice

On 11 November, Ebert's representative, Matthias Erzberger, signed the armistice. This was the formal agreement between Germany and the Allies to end the First World War.

This was the first major decision of the government. The terms of the peace, the Treaty of Versailles, were to become a permanent burden to the new Republic (see page 17).

Setting up the Weimar Republic

The nine months from November 1918 to July 1919 were uneasy for the new Republic whilst a new government was put in place. Ebert took several steps to increase people's confidence in the new Republic.

- Ebert arranged for the civil servants* who had helped [← people working for the government] run Germany under the Kaiser to stay in office. They were instructed to work alongside soldiers' and workers' councils, where local people had set these up. This ensured that the state would keep running – for example, collecting taxes and running public services such as schools.

- He reassured General Groener that the army would not be reformed. Officers kept their ranks. In return, Groener agreed to use the German army to help keep the new Republic in power.

- Ebert also reassured leaders of industry, like the coal and shipping entrepreneur Hugo Stinnes, that the new Republic would not confiscate land or factories and that there would be no nationalisation (state control) of private industries. This helped ensure that businesses and the economy continued to operate.

- Finally, Ebert won the support of the trade unions*. He promised their leader, Carl Legien, that the new Republic would try to achieve an eight-hour working day.

Despite Ebert's efforts, some extreme political parties were still dissatisfied. Demonstrations, and even riots, were common in the major cities. Germany was still on the edge of anarchy.

Still, Ebert had achieved a fragile control, which lasted long enough to agree a new constitution for the new republic.

Key terms

Civil servant*

Somebody who works for the government in some way.

Trade unions*

Groups of workers formed to protect the rights and interests of workers in various occupations.

Source C

A German poster from December 1918. The large figure represents the new Republic. The writing says 'Anarchy Brings Unrest and Hunger'.

Activities

1. By 1918, the First World War had weakened the German government. Look at page 9 and find information that shows the weakness of the government. Write down one example from the text, Figure 1.1, Source A and Interpretation 1.

2. The German revolution was a relatively peaceful transfer of power from the Kaiser's Second Reich to the new republic. Hold a debate to discuss who deserves the credit for this. Make a quarter of your class the Kaiser, a quarter Scheidemann, a quarter Groener and a quarter Ebert. Each group should argue that their person, not the others, deserves the credit.

3. After the debate, write a paragraph saying who you think deserves credit for the relatively peaceful transfer of power.

The National Assembly

The Council of People's Representatives, which took control of Germany in November 1918, was only temporary. Ebert announced that there would be national elections to select a National Assembly. The job of the National Assembly would be to create a new constitution for Germany.

↖ Set of rules

The elections took place on 19 January 1919. They were a success – 82% of the electorate* voted. Moderate parties gained most of the seats: the SPD won 40% and the Centre Party won 20%.

The National Assembly met for the first time in February 1919. Because there was so much unrest and violence in Berlin, they had to meet in the more peaceful town of Weimar, about 250 km away. It took six months to reach an agreement.

On 31 July, the National Assembly agreed a new constitution, by 262 votes to 75. The new republic, now governed by the constitution agreed in Weimar, became known as the Weimar Republic.

> **Key term**
>
> **Electorate***
>
> People who are allowed to vote in an election.

The Weimar Constitution

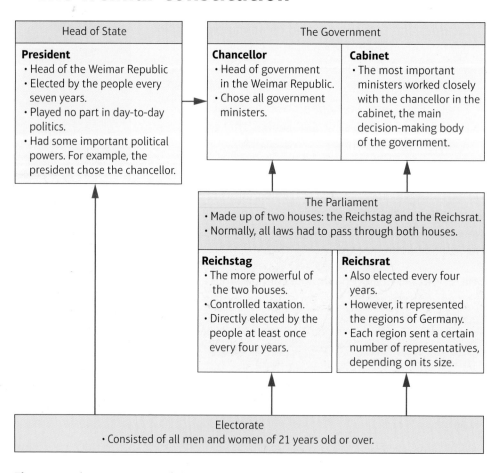

Figure 1.2 The constitution of the Weimar Republic.

Head of State

President
- Head of the Weimar Republic
- Elected by the people every seven years.
- Played no part in day-to-day politics.
- Had some important political powers. For example, the president chose the chancellor.

The Government

Chancellor
- Head of government in the Weimar Republic.
- Chose all government ministers.

Cabinet
- The most important ministers worked closely with the chancellor in the cabinet, the main decision-making body of the government.

The Parliament
- Made up of two houses: the Reichstag and the Reichsrat.
- Normally, all laws had to pass through both houses.

Reichstag
- The more powerful of the two houses.
- Controlled taxation.
- Directly elected by the people at least once every four years.

Reichsrat
- Also elected every four years.
- However, it represented the regions of Germany.
- Each region sent a certain number of representatives, depending on its size.

Electorate
- Consisted of all men and women of 21 years old or over.

The strengths and weaknesses of the Weimar Constitution

The strengths of the constitution

1 **Democratic**. Article 1 of the constitution confirmed that Germany was to be a democracy.

- For the first time in Germany, women were able to vote as well as men.
- The voting age was reduced from 25 to 21.

This was more democratic than Germany under the Kaiser, or Britain at that time.

The Reichstag was elected under a system of **proportional representation**. This was meant to make sure that even the smaller parties had a fair share of seats in the Reichstag. Every party was allocated one representative for each 60,000 votes in its favour.

2 **Checks and balances**. The constitution was carefully constructed so that no one person or one group could have too much power.

- The **president** had the power to choose the chancellor – usually the leader of the largest party.

The president could also dismiss the Reichstag, call new elections and even assume control of the army. Every seven years, the **electorate** could change the president.

- The **chancellor** decided which laws should be passed, though under normal circumstances, these only became law if the majority of the **Reichstag** and **Reichsrat** voted for them.
- The **Reichstag** was the more powerful house of the German parliament – for example, it controlled taxation. However, the **Reichsrat** could delay any new laws passed by the Reichstag, unless the Reichstag overruled it by a two-thirds majority.
- **Central government** (the president, chancellor, Reichstag and Reichsrat) had more power than it did under the Kaiser. However, some traditional powers were retained by **local government**. Each of the 18 regions of Germany, (such as Prussia and Bavaria) kept its own local parliament, called a **land** (plural **Länder**), which controlled key services such as police, courts and schools.

Source D

A photograph, taken on 6 February 1919, showing the official opening of the National Assembly by Friedrich Ebert.

The weaknesses of the constitution

1 **Coalition government**. Proportional representation meant that many small parties won seats in the Reichstag – there were 29 parties in total during the 1920s. Often, no single party had a clear majority. The only way that governments could be formed was for several parties to join together as coalitions.

   • This meant that coalition partners had to compromise, often resulting in a lack of clear, strong policies.

   • Coalitions frequently argued and fell apart. There were nine coalition governments between 1919 and 1923.

2 **Weakness in a crisis**. The lack of strong, single-party governments was a particular problem during a crisis, when swift, clear decisions were needed. The solution to this was Article 48 of the constitution, which said that, in a crisis, the chancellor could ask the president to pass a necessary law by decree, without the support of the Reichstag.

   • By around 1930, the chancellor regularly relied upon the president to pass laws, rather than relying on votes in the Reichstag, bypassing the democratic rules.

   • This made the constitution seem weak and encouraged people to think that a single, all-powerful leader was better than an elected parliament.

3 **Based on division and violence**. Even though it gave ultimate power to the electorate, there was always a sense that the Weimar Republic was not really the choice of the people.

   • During the German revolution, the government had used force (see Source E). They relied on the army to subdue public riots in Berlin and went off to meet at Weimar.

   • Several parties elected to the Reichstag, such as the nationalists and the communists, were opposed to democracy and openly despised the new constitution.

The Weimar Republic was created out of violence, without real public enthusiasm. It was opposed by extremists and considered flawed by moderates.

Activities

1 Copy the diagram of the Weimar constitution on page 12. Use the text on page 13 to label your diagram and show the functions and powers of each part of the constitution.

2 Draw a picture of weighing scales and write strengths and weaknesses of the Weimar Republic on each side of the scales. Overall, do you think it was a good constitution?

3 Who do you think was satisfied with the new constitution? Who was not?

4 The president of the Weimar Republic could dismiss the Reichstag and call new elections, take control of the army and pass laws by decree, with the support of the chancellor but without the support of the Reichstag. Were these abilities strengths or weaknesses of the constitution?

Source E

A photograph taken at the end of 1918 in Berlin. The building behind the army shows damage caused by rioting.

THINKING HISTORICALLY — Evidence (2b&c)

Different perspectives

Sometimes people living at the time of great events only know part of what is going on. Their knowledge of events is limited; they see only part of the picture.

When people like this leave their accounts of events, the information they leave us is useful, but it may not give accurate evidence about the overall picture.

Consider Sources F, G and Interpretation 2. What impression do they give you about how revolutionary the German revolution was?

Answer the following questions:

1 Sources F and G were produced by people living at the time of the German revolution. What impressions do they give you about how revolutionary the German revolution was?

2 Interpretation 2 was written by a modern historian. What impressions does it give you about how revolutionary the German revolution was?

3 What types of information are Sources F and G based on?

4 What types of information is Interpretation 2 based on?

5 Does Interpretation 2 use information that the people in Sources F and G couldn't have used?

6 Why do you think that later interpretations sometimes reach different conclusions about events from sources from the time?

Source F

From a description by Rosa Levine-Meyer of events she saw in the streets of Munich in April 1919. Levine-Meyer was a communist leader who set up workers' councils in Munich in 1919 to replace the local government.

The streets were filled with workers, armed and unarmed, who marched by in detachment... Lorries loaded with armed workers raced through the town, often greeted with jubilant cheers. The bourgeoisie (the middle classes) had disappeared completely.

Source G

From a description of the German revolution by Anton Pannekoek, a Dutch communist who supported the workers' uprisings in Germany at the end of the First World War, in May 1919.

The result of... the military defeat, was revolution... The masses have destroyed the machinery that crushed them... they have won political liberty... In Germany the workers have done the same as in Russia – formed Workers' and Soldiers' Councils. These councils... are the new instrument of power for the masses... against the organisation of the middle classes.

Interpretation 2

From The Coming of the Third Reich by Richard J. Evans, published in 2004.

Fear and hatred… gun battles, riots and civil unrest… ruled the day in Germany at the end of the First World War. Yet somebody had to take over the reins of power… Radical elements looked to the workers' and soldiers' councils. [But] instead of revolution, Ebert wanted parliamentary democracy… Many ordinary electors in Germany saw voting for the three moderate democratic parties as the best way to prevent the creation of a communist revolution. Not surprisingly, therefore, [in January 1919] the Social Democrats, the Democratic Party and the Centre Party gained an overall majority in the elections to the Constituent Assembly. The constitution which it approved in July 1919 was just a modified version of the [old German constitution] established nearly half a century before.

Exam-style question, Section A

Study Source A on page 9.

Give **two** things you can infer from Source A about how well Germany was being governed in November 1918.   **4 marks**

Exam tip

A good answer will select details from the source, for example, 'civilization lies in ruins', 'its peoples broke, starving, despairing' and 'struggling forward along the paths of anarchy' and will suggest what can be inferred from these details about how well Germany was being governed by the end of 1918.

Summary

- With the First World War coming to an end, the Kaiser abdicated on 9 November 1918. The war ended two days later, on 11 November.
- The legacy of the First World War meant that the Social Democratic Party (SPD) had to work quickly to establish order.
- Despite revolts by extremists and riots in the streets, Ebert and the SPD established a new government and a National Assembly.
- The National Assembly met in Weimar and created a constitution for the Weimar Republic.
- The constitution had strengths: it was democratic and was constructed so that no individual or party could hold all the power.
- But it was also flawed. Being a coalition, it was weak in a crisis and was based on division. This later weakened the Weimar Republic.

Checkpoint

Strengthen

S1 List the ways in which the First World War weakened the German government.

S2 Explain how Ebert kept control of Germany from November 1918 to July 1919.

S3 Describe the key features of the Weimar constitution.

S4 List the strengths and weaknesses of the Weimar constitution.

Challenge

C1 Why did the Kaiser have to abdicate in November 1918?

C2 Despite all the public unrest, how did Germany manage to achieve a relatively peaceful transition of power from the Kaiser's Second Reich to the Weimar Republic?

How confident do you feel about your answers to these questions? If you are unsure, look again at pages 9–10 for C1; pages 10–12 for C2. If you are still unsure about a question, discuss with others or with your teacher.

Unpopularity of the Republic

The Weimar Republic did not formally start until July 1919. However, the politicians who set up and ran the Weimar Republic were the same ones who surrendered at the end of the First World War and accepted an unpopular peace treaty. The Weimar Republic was therefore always linked to surrender and harsh peace treaty terms.

The armistice

On 11 November 1918, just two days after the Kaiser had abdicated, Matthias Erzberger, representing the government of the new republic, signed the armistice – an agreement to stop fighting.

In truth, there was little alternative. By November 1918, Germany was torn apart by social and political unrest and its money and troops were running out (see page 9). On the battlefield, the entry of two million US troops into the war in 1917 had made the Allies much stronger. From August 1918, the German army was in retreat and its defensive fortification, the Hindenburg Line, had been breached. Beginning the new republic with a surrender was not a strong start.

The Treaty of Versailles, 1919

Once the **armistice** was signed, the Allied leaders decided the terms of the peace. The peace treaty was eventually signed in a French palace at Versailles, near Paris, on 28 June 1919.

Peace was popular with the German people, as they had suffered during the war. Even so, the terms of the Treaty of Versailles were very unpopular with the German people, and this also made the Weimar Republic unpopular. There were several reasons why.

The diktat

Most Germans assumed that Germany would be able to negotiate the terms of the peace treaty, but the Allies refused to allow any German representatives to join in the treaty discussions. The treaty was a 'diktat' – meaning the terms were imposed, not agreed. Germany had 15 days to make comments. The Germans were bitterly opposed to the treaty terms and asked for concessions. All were refused.

Source A

A German poster from 1931. It advertises a NSDAP rally and shows a German figure in handcuffs labelled 'Versailles'.

War guilt

Article 231 of the treaty stated that Germany had caused the war. Germany did not agree. War guilt meant that, since they were to blame for the war, Germany had to pay reparations – compensation – to the victorious nations. To prevent Germany starting another war in the future, the Allies also insisted on reductions in Germany's armed forces and territory. Germans hated the war guilt clause.

The terms of the Treaty of Versailles

Germany had to pay reparations to the Allies

- In 1921, reparations were eventually fixed at 136,000 million marks (£6.6 billion).

Germany lost all its colonies

- The 11 German colonies in Africa and the Far East were given to victorious countries as 'mandates' – territories to look after.

German military strength was cut

- The army was limited to 100,000 men, with no heavy artillery, to be used only within Germany.

- The navy was limited to six battleships, six cruisers, 12 destroyers and 12 torpedo boats. No submarines were allowed. The rest of the fleet was destroyed.

- No air force was allowed. The existing air force was destroyed.

- The Rhineland – the German land which bordered France – was demilitarised, which meant that the German army was not allowed in. Allied troops were stationed there until 1930.

Germany lost land

- Alsace and Lorraine were lost to France.

- Eupen and Malmedy were lost to Belgium.

- Posen and West Prussia were lost to Poland.

  - The loss of Posen and West Prussia put a million Germans under Polish rule. It also divided Germany in two, cutting off East Prussia from the rest of the country.

- Plebiscites (public votes) had to take place in other areas, to decide whether they should leave Germany.

  - Upper Silesia voted to become part of Poland.

  - Northern Schleswig decided to become part of Denmark.

- The German port of Danzig was made an international city – not governed by Germany.

- The output of the rich Saar coalfields was also to go to France for 15 years.

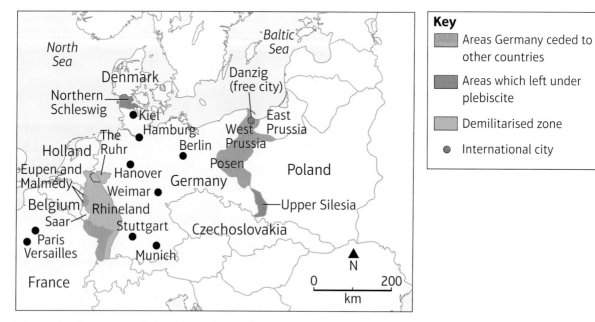

Figure 1.3 Germany and the Treaty of Versailles.

- Altogether, Germany lost:
- 10% of its population and 13% of its European territory
- all its overseas property and investments
- almost 50% of its iron and 15% of its coal reserves.

Dolchstoss – the stab in the back

Another reason the Treaty of Versailles was unpopular was because the German people didn't believe their army had been defeated in the war. Though it was in retreat by November 1918, the German army was not defeated. Critics of the treaty said the army was betrayed by politicians – that they were 'stabbed in the back' (Dolchstoss). Even Ebert, the chancellor of the new Republic greeted the German Army in December 1918 with the words 'Your sacrifice and deeds are without parallel. No enemy defeated you!'

Source B

A poster from 1924 showing a German soldier being 'stabbed in the back'.

Source C

From an article in *Deutsche Zeitung*, a German newspaper, 28 June 1919.

```
Vengeance, German nation! Today, in the Hall
of Mirrors at Versailles, a disgraceful
treaty is being signed. Never forget it! On
that spot... German honour is being dragged
to its grave. There will be revenge for the
shame of 1919.
```

The impact of the treaty on the Weimar Republic

The Treaty of Versailles damaged Germany's economy and imposed heavy reparations, so that it could not start another world war. This made the economy of the Weimar Republic weak from the outset.

It also made the Weimar Republic politically weak. The treaty was so harsh that people resented the leaders of the new German republic who signed it. They became known as the '**November Criminals**' because they surrendered in November 1918. From the outset, the Weimar Republic was linked to defeat, humiliation and weakness.

Activities ?

1. Play 'Versailles Volleyball'. Divide the class in half and take it in turns to 'lob' a German grievance about the Treaty of Versailles 'over the net' to the other team until one side fails to give a different grievance – and loses the game. Jot down each grievance as you play.

2. Consider: the diktat, war guilt, reparations, military limits, lost land, the 'stab in the back'. Which was the biggest grievance? Write a brief case for each, then make a choice and justify it.

3. What support can you find on pages 17–19 for the opinions in Interpretation 1?

Interpretation 1

From *The Coming of the Third Reich* by Richard J. Evans, published in 2004.

No one was prepared for the peace terms... All of this was greeted with incredulous horror by the majority of Germans. The sense of outrage and disbelief... was almost universal. Germany's international strength and prestige had been on an upward course since unification in 1871... now, suddenly, Germany had been brutally expelled from the ranks of the Great Powers and covered in what they considered to be undeserved shame. Versailles was condemned as a dictated peace, unilaterally imposed without the possibility of negotiation.

Challenges to the Weimar Republic from the Left and Right

In the National Assembly (see page 12), which created the constitution for the new republic, moderates were in the majority. The **Social Democrats** (SPD) worked with other moderate parties, like the **Democrats** (DDP) and the **Centre Party**, to create the Weimar Republic in 1919. Combined, they had about 80% of seats in the Assembly.

However, there were extreme left-wing and right-wing parties which did not support the Weimar Republic.

Right wing and left wing   Right wing = capitalist

Extreme right-wing groups wanted a return to a strong government, with a strong army, headed by powerful leader, like the Kaiser. They supported capitalism – the private ownership of land and business – and championed families, law and order and traditional values. They tended to place the interests of the nation over the individual. The National Party (DNVP) was the main right-wing party in 1919.

left wing = communist/socialist
Extreme left-wing groups wanted Germany to be controlled by the people. They opposed capitalism and wanted to abolish private ownership of land and business and put them in the hands of workers. They were internationalists who stressed the co-operation, rather than independence, of nations. The German Communist Party (KPD) was the main left-wing party in 1919.

The challenge of the Left and Right in the Reichstag

Although the three main moderate parties had 77% of the seats in the National Assembly, after the elections of 6 June 1920 they had only 45% of the seats in the new Reichstag. The extreme left-wing and right-wing parties had about 20% of seats each. The rest were divided amongst smaller parties. For most of the 1920s, the moderate centre parties struggled to form majority coalitions, whilst being constantly attacked in the Reichstag by extremist politicians from the left and right wings.

Interpretation 2

From *Nazism and War* by Richard Bessel, published in 2004.

The Social Democratic politicians, into whose lap the German government fell in 1918, didn't have widespread support. Instead, they faced a bitter, suffering population, filled with unrealistic ideas about what peace could bring and divided about… the road ahead.

Activity   ?

1 Study Interpretation 1 and Interpretation 2, which both describe the political situation around 1920. What do they agree on, and what information is found in only one of the extracts?

The main parties of the Weimar Republic

Extremist	Moderate Parties				Extremist	
KPD	SPD	DDP	ZP	DVP	DNVP	NSDAP
Communist party	Social Democrats	Democrats	Centre Party	People's party	National Party	Nazi Party
Extreme left wing	Moderate left wing	Moderate left wing	Moderate	Moderate right wing	Right wing	Extreme right wing
Opposed the Weimar Republic	Supported Weimar Republic	Supported Weimar Republic	Supported Weimar Republic	Sometimes supported Republic	Grudgingly accepted Republic	Opposed Weimar Republic
Supported by workers and some middle classes	Supported by workers and middle classes	Backed by intellectual middle classes	Conservatives. Originally the party of the Catholic Church	Backed by upper middle classes	Landowners, the wealthy and big business	Founded in 1920, eventual main party of Germany in the 1930s

LEFT   RIGHT

Figure 1.4 The main parties of the Weimar Republic.

The challenge of the left and right outside the Reichstag

The Weimar Republic also faced challenges from the left and right outside the Reichstag.

The Spartacist Revolt – a left-wing uprising

The German Communist Party (KPD) was set up in December 1918. It was backed by the Soviet Union and so was well funded. It soon had 33 daily newspapers and 400,000 members. The Communists were supported by the Spartacist League. The Spartacist League were extreme socialists from the USPD, the Independent Socialist Party based in Berlin. They named themselves after the head of a slaves' revolt in Ancient Rome – Spartacus. The Spartacists supported the communists, and were led by Rosa Luxemburg (known as 'Red Rosa') and Karl Liebknecht.

On 4 January 1919, Ebert sacked Emil Eichhorn, the police chief in Berlin, who was popular with the workers. On the next day, thousands of workers took to the streets in protest. The Spartacists saw this as their chance to undermine the government. They called for an uprising and a general strike in Berlin and, on 6 January, over 100,000 workers took to the streets. They seized the government's newspaper and telegraph offices. The Weimar government was losing control of the capital.

The Freikorps

Chancellor Ebert needed to put down the Spartacist rebels. However, so soon after the war, the German armed forces (the Reichswehr) was in no shape to put down the revolt alone, so Ebert turned to a new force.

Thousands of soldiers released from the army had returned to Germany in November 1918, but had kept their weapons. Many were right wing and strongly opposed to the communists. Ebert ordered Reichswehr officers to organise these demobilised soldiers into Freikorps (Free Corps) units. It is estimated that the Freikorps numbered 250,000 men by March 1919.

Source D

A Spartacist poster from the 1920s. The Spartacist champion of the people slays the three-headed monster – the army, big business and landowners – considered by the extreme left wing to be oppressing the people.

The end of the Spartacist Revolt

As the Spartacist Revolt grew, Ebert turned the Freikorps on the rioters. The mainly unarmed workers were no match for them. By 13 January, the rebels had been driven off the streets. On 16 January, Luxemburg and Liebknecht were arrested and killed by Freikorps officers. Liebknecht was shot. Luxemburg was struck on the head with a rifle butt, shot in the head and her body dumped in a canal. For the time being, the left-wing communist rebellion had been suppressed.

The Kapp Putsch – a right-wing uprising

By 1920, Ebert's government were struggling to control the Freikorps. In March 1920, Freikorps units near Berlin were due to be disbanded. Fearing unemployment, they turned their arms against the republic. Five thousand armed men marched on Berlin. When Ebert ordered General Seeckt, the head of the Reichswehr, to resist the rebels, he replied, 'Reichswehr does not fire upon Reichswehr'. Soon, the rebels controlled the city. They put forward a nationalist politician, Wolfgang Kapp, as a figurehead leader. They declared a new government of Germany and invited the Kaiser to return from exile.

In fear for their lives, members of the real government fled to Weimar and then to Stuttgart. Unable to put the revolt down by force, they urged people not to co-operate and instead go on strike. Many workers obliged, as they had socialist leanings and no desire to see the Kaiser return. Essential services – gas, electricity, water, transport – stopped and the capital ground to a halt.

After four days, Kapp realised he could not govern. He fled, but was caught and put in prison, where he later died. The rebellion collapsed and the Weimar ministers returned.

The challenge of ongoing political violence 1919–23

Even after the defeat of the Spartacist and Kapp uprisings, political challenges to the Weimar Republic continued from the left and right wings. One challenge involved a series of political assassinations.

- **Hugo Haasse**, one of Ebert's Council of People's Representatives, was murdered in 1919.
- **Matthias Erzberger**, the politician who signed the surrender to the Allies in 1918, was shot and killed in August 1921.
- **Walther Rathenau**, the Weimar foreign minister, was machine-gunned to death in Berlin in June 1922.

In all, between 1919 and 1922 there were 376 political murders, mostly of left-wing or moderate politicians. Not a single right-wing murderer was convicted and executed, while ten left-wing assassins were. Judges sympathetic to the right wing even undermined the Weimar Republic in the courts.

Activities

1. Choose three people from your class to talk – without hesitation, repetition or deviation – about the Spartacist Revolt, the Kapp Putsch and the Freikorps. The person who can talk for the longest wins. Afterwards, list the key facts about each one.
2. Using pages 20–22, write three policies which could have been put forward by Communists, Social Democrats and Nationalists.

Amidst all this political violence, most political parties hired armed men to guard their meetings. They mainly recruited ex-soldiers who were unemployed.

- The KPD set up a private army called the Rotfrontkämpfer (**Red Front Fighters**).
- The DNVP were supported by the Stahlhelm (**Steel Helmets**).
- Even the moderate SPD had the Reichsbanner Schwartz-Rot-Gold (**Black Red Gold Flag**).

At first, these private political armies were for protection, but their presence often caused political meetings and marches to become violent.

The Weimar Republic therefore staggered through the years 1919–22, plagued by challenges from left-wing and right-wing extremists inside and outside the Reichstag. Things became even worse in 1923.

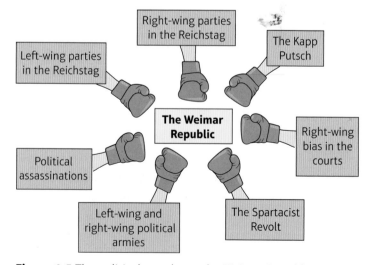

Figure 1.5 The political attacks on the Weimar Republic.

The challenges of 1923

French occupation of the Ruhr

Germany's biggest problem was that its government was bankrupt – its reserves of gold had all been spent in the war. The Treaty of Versailles made things worse. It deprived Germany of wealth-earning areas, such as the coalfields in Silesia. It also made the German government pay reparations. Germany asked for reductions, but some Allied countries, especially France, needed money to pay war debts to the USA. With no gold reserves and falling income, by 1923 Germany could no longer pay reparations.

In December 1922, Germany failed to send coal to France from the Ruhr coalfields, as they were supposed to do under the reparations arrangement. In retaliation, the French sent troops into the German industrial area of the Ruhr in January 1923 (see the map on page 18). They confiscated raw materials, manufactured goods and industrial machinery. The German government urged passive resistance – workers went on strike and there was even some sabotage. The French responded by arresting those who obstructed them and bringing in their own workers.

The Germans bitterly resented what the French had done. However, many Germans also resented the failure of the Weimar Republic to resist the French, even though, realistically, they had no choice. Germany's reduced troop numbers of 100,000 were no match for the 750,000 soldiers in the French army.

The occupation of the Ruhr crippled Germany, as it contained many factories and around 80% of German coal, iron and steel reserves. The disruption increased Germany's debts, increased unemployment and worsened the shortage of goods.

Inflation and hyperinflation

These shortages in early 1923 meant that the price of things went up – this is called **inflation**. People had to pay more money to get what they needed. Government decisions made things worse.

The government needed money to pay their debts, but unemployment and failing factories meant they received less money from taxes. During 1919–23,

Source E

A poster from Germany in 1923. The figure represents France. The caption reads 'Hands off the Ruhr area!'

Hände weg vom Ruhrgebiet!

government income was only a quarter of what was required. So, unable to gain more money from taxes, the government printed more money. In 1923, the government had 300 paper mills and 2,000 printing shops dedicated to printing more bank notes.

Initially, printing extra money made it easier for the government to pay reparations – but it also made inflation even worse. It was a vicious circle: the more prices rose, the more money was printed and this made prices rise again. By 1923, prices reached spectacular heights (see the table below). This extreme inflation is called **hyperinflation**.

Price of a loaf of bread	
1919	1 mark
1922	100 marks
1923	200,000 billion marks

The effects of hyperinflation

The results of hyperinflation were complex.

1 **Normal living became impossible.** Printing presses could not produce enough currency. People had to pin money to letters, because stamps were useless. They had to carry bundles of money in baskets and even wheelbarrows. Many workers were paid twice a day, so they could rush out and buy goods before prices rose even further. Some shops refused to take money at all, asking for payment in kind (swapping goods). Some people raided shops because they couldn't afford food.

2 **Everyone suffered from shortages.** This was because German marks became worthless for importing goods. In 1918, buying £1 worth of foreign goods cost 20 marks; by November 1923, buying £1 worth of foreign goods cost 20 billion marks. Foreign suppliers refused to accept German marks for goods, so imports dried up and shortages of food and other goods got worse – for everyone.

3 **People with savings** were hit hardest – those with money in bank accounts, insurance policies or pensions. Their saved money became worthless. The middle classes were the worst affected.

However, not everybody suffered. There were people who benefitted from inflation.

- People who had loans, or who took out loans, found that the value of the money they owed went down. For example, some big businessmen borrowed money and profited because the value of their debts went down.

- Other people hoarded goods and then sold them for a large profit as prices went up.

- Foreign visitors also benefitted, as the value of their own currency rose against the German mark, so they could buy much more with their money. German people bitterly resented people who made money out of their suffering.

Source F

A photograph of children using stacks of bank notes as building blocks in Germany in 1923.

The damage done

After August 1923, a new chancellor, Gustav Stresemann, found solutions to some of the problems of 1923 (see page 27). By this point, however, the political and economic turmoil from 1918 to 1923 had done its damage.

- The Weimar Republic was shown to be weak. It had to be rescued by Freikorps in 1919 and workers' strikes in 1920. Government forces had killed thousands of Germans in order to stay in power.

- All Germans had suffered. Most blamed the Weimar Republic for their suffering. The middle classes, which would normally be the bedrock of the republic, suffered most.

- Extremist parties, with private armies hostile to the republic, had gained in strength.

Activities ?

1   Working with a partner, create a list of reasons why the German government had run out of money by December 1922. (Hint: look back through the book to add to your list.)

2   Outline the reasons for and effects of the French occupation of the Ruhr.

3   Write the following list on small cards: fall in value of pensions, shortage of industrial goods, government bankruptcy, fall in value of savings, inflation, reparations, occupation of the Ruhr, printing more money, loss of land after Versailles.

    a   Organise the cards into causes and effects. Draw lines to link causes and their effects. (Note that some cards may be both a cause of one thing and an effect of another.)

    b   What does the resulting diagram tell you about the causes of the bankruptcy of the German government?

    c   What does it tell you about the causes of the social and economic problems of the German people?

THINKING HISTORICALLY   Interpretations 2a

The work of the historian

Historians do not aim to tell us about the whole past – they need to choose what aspects of the past to investigate. When doing this, they have to select what is important in order not to overload their work with detail. For example, an overview history of the creation of the Weimar Republic might not include witness statements from rioters on the streets, but a work about how the Spartacist Revolt was defeated might contain many such witness statements.

Political turmoil in the Weimar Republic 1918–23 – some key information:

55% of German troops in the First World War were killed or wounded.	The price of bread was 200,000 million times higher in 1923 than it was in 1919.	Money put into savings in 1919 was worthless by 1923.
In 1920, Freikorps shot or arrested people who demonstrated in the streets.	Germans believed that their army had been 'stabbed in the back' by the November Criminals.	French occupation of the Ruhr disrupted German factories there.
The Allies declared that Germany was to blame for the start of the First World War.	In late 1923, if you ordered a coffee for 5,000 marks you could be charged 8,000 by the time you drank it.	Germany was told to pay £6.6bn in reparations as compensation to the Allies.

Which of the above pieces of information would be best suited for investigating the following issues? Write out each of the four questions below and then choose up to four pieces of information from the table for each.

1   How fair were the terms of the Treaty of Versailles?

2   Why was there so much unrest in Germany at the end of 1918?

3   What were the main causes of suffering in Germany 1919–23?

4   What were the effects of hyperinflation in 1923?

With a partner, discuss the following questions and write down your thoughts:

1   Why is it important to be selective about the information that you put in your historical writing?

2   How important are the questions the historian asks in deciding what information is included in their writing?

Exam-style question, Section A

Explain why there were economic problems in the Weimar Republic from 1919 to 1923.

You may use the following in your answer:

- reparations
- the French occupation of the Ruhr.

You **must** also use information of your own. **12 marks**

Exam tip

A good answer will:

- include several factors that caused economic problems
- contain detailed information about each factor and its economic effects
- explain why each factor caused economic problems.

Summary

- The Treaty of Versailles and the 'stab in the back' theory made the Weimar Republic unpopular after 1919.
- From 1919 to 1923, the Weimar Republic was attacked by extreme left-wing and right-wing political groups, inside and outside the Reichstag.
- Examples of these attacks include the Spartacist Revolt and the Kapp Putsch.
- 1923 brought new challenges for the Weimar Republic, notably the French occupation of the Ruhr and hyperinflation.

Checkpoint

Strengthen

S1 List the terms of the Treaty of Versailles which made the Weimar Republic unpopular.

S2 Describe the causes, events and reasons for the failure of the Spartacist Revolt and the Kapp Putsch.

S3 What were the reasons for, and the effects of, the French occupation of the Ruhr?

S4 What were the reasons for, and the effects of, hyperinflation?

Challenge

C1 What were the typical beliefs and policies of left-wing and right-wing political groups?

C2 Explain the reasons for political instability in the Weimar Republic, 1919–23.

C3 Explain the reasons for economic instability in the Weimar Republic, 1919–23.

How confident do you feel about your answers to these questions? If you are unsure look again at page 20 for C1, pages 21–22 for C2, pages 23–24 for C3. If you are still unsure about a question, join together with others and discuss a joint answer. Your teacher can provide hints.

In August 1923, President Ebert appointed Gustav Stresemann as his new chancellor and foreign secretary. Stresemann resigned the chancellorship in November 1923, but remained as foreign secretary until 1929.

Stresemann's strategy

Stresemann's most important work was in economic and foreign policy (see details below). However, his main objective was to make the political situation in Germany more stable. He hoped that by stabilising the economy and regaining respect for Germany in foreign affairs, Germans would feel more content with the Weimar Republic. This way, he hoped to unite most Germans behind moderate political parties, and reduce the support for extreme political parties like the National Socialist German Workers' Party (NSDAP) and the Communist Party (see Source A).

Source A

From a speech by Stresemann, describing his support for middle-of-the-road policies in 1924.

I regard it as my duty, as a party man and as a minister, to do all I can to unite the German people for these decisions, and not to force upon them the choice: bourgeois or socialist.

Reasons for economic recovery

Rentenmark

In November 1923, Stresemann set up a new state-owned bank, the **Rentenbank**. This issued new currency – the **Rentenmark**. The supply of these notes was strictly limited. Their value was tied to the price of gold and they were backed by German industrial plants and agricultural land. Therefore, the currency had real value. Unlike the old mark, people trusted it.

Later, in August 1924, a newly independent national bank, the **Reichsbank**, was given control of this new currency.

It was renamed the **Reichsmark** and was backed by Germany's gold reserves. German money was now trusted at home and abroad, and hyperinflation was at an end.

This was a much stronger basis for the recovery of German businesses and improvements to employment. Unfortunately, it could not bring back the losses of those people ruined by hyperinflation.

The Dawes Plan, 1924

Charles G. Dawes, an American banker, had been asked by the Allies to resolve Germany's non-payment of reparations. In April 1924, Stresemann agreed to the Dawes Plan. Under this plan:

- reparations were temporarily reduced to £50 million per year
- US banks agreed to give loans to German industry. They loaned $25 billion between 1924 and 1930.

This combined package reassured the Allies that they would get their reparations payments. Stresemann had already called off German workers' passive resistance in the Ruhr. As a result, the French agreed to leave the Ruhr.

All of this improved the Weimar Republic's economy, much to the benefit of working-class and middle-class Germans.

- Industrial output doubled between 1923 and 1928, passing pre-First World War levels.
- Employment, trade and income from taxation increased.

Most Germans were reassured and this strengthened the Weimar Republic politically. However, there were drawbacks.

- The extreme political parties were furious that Germany had again agreed to pay reparations.
- Furthermore, the fragile economic recovery depended on American loans (see Source B on page 28).

Activities ?

In pairs, read the following statement by Streseman in 1929: 'The economic position only flourishes on the surface. Germany dances on a volcano. If loans are called in by the USA, a large section of our economy will collapse'.

1 List the economic changes made from 1923 to 1929 that were permanent and secure.

2 List those that depended on US loans.

3 Explain how far Stresemann was correct. How dependent on US loans was Germany?

Source B

A right-wing cartoon published in 1923. The figure behind the curtain represents the USA. Wall Street was the US financial centre. The caption says 'Here is your enemy'.

The Young Plan, 1929

Five years later, Stresemann made further progress with reparations when he agreed the Young Plan. This plan was put forward by a committee in August 1929, set up by the Allies, and was headed by an American banker called Owen Young.

The Young Plan reduced the total reparations debt from £6.6 billion to £2 billion. Moreover, Germany was given a further 59 years to pay.

The extreme political parties were incensed. The increasingly well-known leader of the Nazi Party (see page 42), Adolf Hitler, said that extending the length of payments was 'passing on the penalty to the unborn'.

There were definitely drawbacks:

- The annual payments were still £50 million per year.
- Furthermore, they now stretched out until 1988.

However, it was a sensible measure.

- Lower reparations payments allowed the government to lower taxes on ordinary German people.

- Lower taxes released public spending power. This boosted German industry and created more jobs; these jobs boosted spending power and this boosted industry and employment again. This is known as a 'virtuous cycle' of economic growth.
- Finally, linked to the Young Plan, the French agreed to leave the Rhineland in 1930.
- All this increased the confidence of Germans in the Weimar Republic.

Most Germans saw the Young Plan as a success for Stresemann. A referendum, held in 1929, resulted in 35 million Germans in favour of the Young Plan – about 85% of those who voted.

Recovery in foreign relations

Just like his economic policies, Stresemann's work in foreign affairs was also intended to strengthen the confidence of German people in the Weimar Republic.

The Locarno Pact, 1925

On 1 December 1925, Stresemann signed the Locarno Pact. This was a treaty between Germany, Britain, France, Italy and Belgium.

The key thing about Locarno was that, unlike Versailles, it was agreed by Germany, on equal terms with the other main powers – it was not imposed upon Germany.

- Germany accepted its new 1919 border with France, and France promised peace with Germany.
- Germany and the Allies agreed that the Rhineland would be permanently demilitarised (made free of troops).
- The five powers agreed to open talks about German membership of the League of Nations (see below).

Stresemann saw this as a triumph.

- It made war in Europe less likely. Stresemann was even given the Nobel Peace Prize in 1926.
- Germany was also being treated as an equal. This was a boost to the prestige of the Weimar Republic and increased the confidence of many Germans in the moderate political parties who supported Stresemann.

But not all political parties in Germany agreed – some extreme parties resented that the hated Versailles borders had been confirmed.

Source C

A picture from the front of the German magazine *Kladderadatsch* in 1926. The hands represent Germany. The tombstone is labelled Treaty of Versailles. The figures on the top represent Germany's wartime enemies.

The League of Nations

At the end of the First World War, the Allies had founded the League of Nations. This was a new international body in which powerful countries discussed ways of solving the world's problems without resorting to war. Initially, Germany was excluded. In September 1926, Stresemann persuaded the other great powers to accept Germany as a member. Germany was given a place on the League of Nations Council, which took the most important decisions of the League.

Again, this was a boost to the moderate parties who supported Stresemann. It also boosted the confidence of most Germans in the Weimar Republic. However, not all political parties agreed. To some, the League was a symbol of the hated Treaty of Versailles and they wanted nothing to do with it. However, Stresemann's view was different (see Source D).

Source D

An extract from Stresemann's speech on Germany's entry into the League of Nations, 1926.

```
... the League is the product of the treaties
of 1919. Many disputes have arisen between
the League and Germany because of these
treaties. I hope that our co-operation with
the League will make it easier in future to
discuss these questions.
```

Kellogg-Briand Pact

In August 1928, Germany and 61 other countries signed the Kellogg-Briand Pact. This pact promised that states would not use war to achieve foreign policy aims. It was the work of two French and US foreign ministers, and was named after them. The USA was not in the League of Nations and saw this as a way that the country could assist peace.

This was another step forward for Germany in foreign affairs.

- In contrast to the Treaty of Versailles, it showed that Germany was now included amongst the main powers, not dictated to by them.

- It was also another sign that the Weimar Republic was now a respected, stable state.

- This was another boost to the prestige of the Weimar Republic in the eyes of the German public. It increased confidence that the moderate political parties could be trusted to make Germany strong.

However, not all Germans agreed. The Kellogg-Briand Pact did nothing to remove the hated terms of the Treaty of Versailles, which still restricted German strength with reparations, lost land and military restrictions (see Source E).

Source E

A 1929 cartoon, published in Germany, entitled 'Tying Your Friend in Knots'. Briand, the French foreign minister, is on the left, and greets Stresemann as the US president looks on.

The impact on domestic politics

Stresemann's strategy had been to remove the grievances and hardships of the German people, to cut support for extreme parties and reach agreements with other powers, so he could negotiate changes to the Versailles Treaty. The impact of his successes on German politics is clear. Figure 1.6 shows that support for moderate political parties rose and support for extreme parties fell. As a result, by 1929, the Weimar Republic was a more secure and stable state. Source F and Interpretation 1 describe the improvements that had occurred.

Election results to the Reichstag

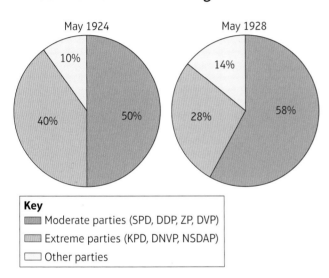

Figure 1.6 A breakdown of the election results.

Germany's growing confidence in the Weimar Republic was strengthened in 1925, when Friedrich Ebert, president of the republic, died. He was one of the Social Democrats who led the revolution against the Kaiser and was seen as one of the 'November Criminals'. He was replaced by Paul von Hindenburg, the former field marshal of the Kaiser's army. Hindenburg reassured the middle class and gave the Weimar Republic a strong figurehead.

However, on 3 October 1929, after six years as foreign minister, Stresemann had a heart attack and died. The loss of his moderate policies was a severe blow to the Weimar Republic. Worse still, a world economic crisis followed soon after. This unleashed a new wave of extreme economic and political pressures on the Weimar Republic.

Source F

A German journalist, writing in 1929.

In comparison with what we expected after Versailles, Germany has raised herself up. It now shoulders the terrific burden of that peace in a way we should never have thought possible. The bad feeling of Versailles has been conquered.

Interpretation 1

From a history textbook for schools, published in Britain in 2015.

As the economy improved, so social conditions stabilised and political violence died down. Between 1924 and 1929, no major political figures were assassinated. The Weimar government had been in power for long enough for many people to accept that it was now the political system in Germany – as long as things continued to improve. Support for extremist parties (both left wing and right wing) reduced... Coalition governments were still the norm, although they changed less often: between 1924 and1929, there were just six different coalitions. Stresemann's influence was vital to this. However, none of the weaknesses of the constitution had been resolved. And in 1929, Stresemann died.

Activities ?

1. Hold a class debate about whether you agree with this statement: 'Between 1923 and 1929, Gustav Stresemann solved the problems of the Weimar Republic'. One half of the class should support the statement and the other half should oppose it.

2. On the basis of your debate, create a table, like the one started below, to show the ways in which Stresemann's policies between 1923 and 1929 helped Germany to become more stable.

	How the policy helped	Ways in which it didn't
1923 Rentenmark		
(next policy)		

3. Using your table, write a paragraph to describe how far you think that, by 1929, the Weimar Republic had recovered from its earlier problems of 1919–23.

Exam-style question, Section B

Study Source B (page 28) and Source F (page 31).

How useful are Source B and Source F for an enquiry into the recovery of the Weimar Republic between 1923 and 1929?

Explain your answer, using Source B, Source F and your knowledge of the historical context. **8 marks**

Exam tip

A good answer will consider:

- how useful the information in each source is for this particular enquiry
- how the provenance (i.e. the type of source, its origin, author or purpose) of each source affects how useful it is
- how knowledge of history at that time affects a judgement of how useful each source is.

Summary

- As finance minister, Stresemann introduced a new currency, which ended hyperinflation in the Weimar Republic and aided economic recovery in Germany.
- The Dawes Plan and Young Plan reduced the burden of reparations on the Weimar Republic.
- Under Stresemann as foreign minister, the Locarno Pact, membership of the League of Nations and Kellogg-Briand Pact marked the return of Germany as a world power, thus enabling the Weimar Republic to become a more stable state.
- However, not all the problems of the Weimar Republic were solved. In 1929, Stresemann died and, worse still, later that year a new economic crisis took place.

Checkpoint

Strengthen

S1 Describe the introduction of the Rentenmark, the Dawes Plan and Young Plan.

S2 Describe Germany's part in the Locarno Pact, League of Nations and Kellogg-Briand Pact.

S3 What economic improvements were there in the Weimar Republic from 1924 to 1929?

S4 Explain why there was improved political stability in the Weimar Republic from 1924 to 1929.

Challenge

C1 Explain why the Weimar Republic became more stable from 1924 to 1929.

C2 Explain the reasons for an underlying instability in the Weimar Republic in 1929.

C3 Write a balanced evaluation of how stable the Weimar Republic was in 1929.

How confident do you feel about your answers to these questions? If you are unsure, , look again at pages 27–29 for S1 and S3, pages 29–30 for S2, and page 31 for S4, C1, C2, and C3. If you are still unsure about a question, join together with others and discuss a joint answer. Your teacher can give you hints.

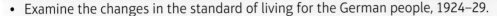

Learning outcomes

- Examine the changes in the standard of living for the German people, 1924–29.
- Understand changes for women in the Weimar Republic.
- Understand cultural changes in the Weimar Republic.

Changes in the standard of living

Living standards suffered as a result of the economic problems between 1918 and 1923. However, there were gradual social improvements after 1924. Many of these were funded by the Weimar government.

Unemployment and unemployment insurance

Unemployment was a social problem in the early years of the Weimar Republic. In 1924, over 4% of the total possible workforce was unemployed. However, there were gradual improvements.

Unemployment	
1926	2 million
1928	1.3 million

Furthermore, help for the unemployed improved. The Unemployment Insurance Act of 1927 charged 16,400,000 workers 3% of their wages and in return provided an average of 60 marks per week in unemployment and sickness benefits if they fell out of work.

Work and wages

For those in work, wages and working conditions improved. Though the length of the working week shortened (see the table below), real wages (the value of goods that wages bought) rose by 25% from 1925 to 1928.

Average hours in a working week	
1925	50 hours
1927	46 hours

Housing

Housing also improved. By 1923, there was a shortage of one million homes in Germany. In 1925, a 15% rent tax was introduced to fund building associations. From 1925 to 1929, private companies built 37,000 new homes, while the new building associations built 64,000 homes. One association alone, GEHAG, built almost 10,000 new houses in Berlin. There was still a housing shortage, but it had eased by 1928.

Other improvements

War veterans were offered help. Under the 1920 Reich Pension Law, pensions were paid throughout the 1920s to 750,000 war veterans, 400,000 war widows and 200,000 parents of dead servicemen.

Education improved and more young people's aspirations were met. The number of students in higher education before the First World War was 70,000. By 1928, this had increased to 110,000.

An improvement in the standard of living?

Improvements in social conditions in the Weimar Republic were fragile. Employment remained insecure and the loss of savings during the inflation of 1923 still caused hardship. Also, not everyone was pleased by the social improvements in 1924–28 (see Interpretation 1).

Interpretation 1

From the History Teachers' Association *Modern History Guide*, published in 2007.

Working people actually improved their situation with better real wages, unemployment insurance and lower working hours. What this did, however, was to alienate other groups such as big business, who resented their loss of power and profit, and the lower middle class, who saw their own position threatened by a system which seemed to favour the working class.

Interpretation 2

From an article on women in Weimar Germany, written by Rudiger Grafin in 2009.

Because of women's improved position in the workforce and their newly acquired rights as citizens... women themselves seemed to have changed... Magazines... presented a new generation of women that differed fundamentally from their mothers.

Changes for women in the Weimar Republic

Women in politics

The Social Democrats, who came to power in 1918, believed in giving women the right to vote. Many others agreed. Women had worked hard for the war effort, so there were strong arguments for rewarding women by treating them equally with men. As a result, in November 1918, in the first week of the new Republic, the government gave women the vote and the right to stand for elections.

Women took full advantage of these rights. In the Weimar elections, the turnout of women voters was 90%. By 1932, 112 women had been elected to the Reichstag. In 1932, almost 10% of members were female.

The Weimar Republic also strengthened the rights of women. Article 109 of the new constitution stated that:

- women had equal rights with men
- marriage was an equal partnership, with equal rights on both sides
- women should be able to enter all professions on an equal basis with men.

Women at work

During the First World War, with so many men involved in the fighting, more women went into paid work. By 1918, 75% of women were in work, often doing jobs previously performed only by men.

In some ways, under the Weimar Republic the lives of women returned to the way they had been pre-war. By 1925, for example, only 36% of women were in work – about the same as pre-war levels. Furthermore, women were not treated equally in the workplace, despite Article 109.

- In jobs where women and men did the same work, women were paid, on average, 33% less than men.
- Women were normally expected to give up work once they married.
- Few women entered high-status professions. By 1933, there were only 36 female judges in Germany.

However, there was some progress for women at work.

- The booming retail and service sectors produced plenty of part-time jobs in shops and offices.
- In some more liberal professions, like education and medicine, women made more progress. For example, the number of female doctors rose from 2,500 to about 5,000 between 1925 and 1932.

So, change for women at work was a mixed picture. The limited changes which did take place stirred up some negative feelings. In industry, trade unions were strong and male-dominated. They opposed women workers and equal pay and conditions for those women that did work. They were especially hostile to 'double earners' (married women bringing a second wage into the home).

Women at leisure

For some women, especially young, unmarried working women living in cities, where there were job opportunities, the 1920s brought greater financial independence. Growing up during the war, they were also used to greater social independence. Many of these became 'new women'.

'New women' bought more clothes and went out more. They expressed their independence by their behaviour. They wore short hair, more make-up, more jewellery and more revealing clothes. They smoked and drank more and went out unaccompanied. Some seemed less interested in marriage and families and took advantage of liberal sexual attitudes which had developed during the war.

Source A

A magazine cover from 1925, comparing a woman from the past (in the foreground) with a 'woman of today' (at the back).

Images of these 'new women' became common in advertisements and films, but they were not popular with all Germans. Many Germans – mainly men, but also many women – believed that the growing equality and independence of women threatened to change traditional aspects of society, such as motherhood, family and good housekeeping. As evidence, they pointed out that:

- the birth rate was falling. In 1913, there were 128 live births each year per 1,000 women. By 1925, this had fallen to 80. Many people felt that Germany needed women to be mothers.
- the divorce rate was rising. In 1913, there were 27 divorces each year per 100,000 people. By the 1920s, this had risen to 60. Many people felt that Germany needed women to be wives.

Society divided

These limited improvements for women were a source of worry to many people in Weimar Germany – though some people welcomed them.

For example:

- some women felt liberated by new opportunities and freedoms; however, other women found the expectation that they should change a scary or daunting challenge
- some men accepted changing roles for women, while others thought that the changes were inappropriate; there were some men who even thought that these 'new women' threatened the role of men in society
- conservatives and traditionalists in society complained loudly that women should concentrate on being mothers and wives, and not challenge the male-dominated society (these traditionalists included members of the clergy)
- some people blamed the economic instability in Germany in the 1920s on women upsetting the labour market.

Because of these attitudes, changes for women in the Weimar Republic was the source of many social tensions.

Cultural changes in the Weimar Republic

A variety of factors led to an upsurge in cultural experimentation in Weimar Germany.

Interpretation 3

From *Weimar and Nazi Germany*, by Stephen Lee published in 1996.

The 1920s saw a huge cultural revival in Germany. Indeed, these years have been seen as the greatest period of experimentation in the whole of Germany's history. As things settled down politically, writers and artists had more of a chance to try out new ideas. The results were impressive and spread across all areas of the Arts.

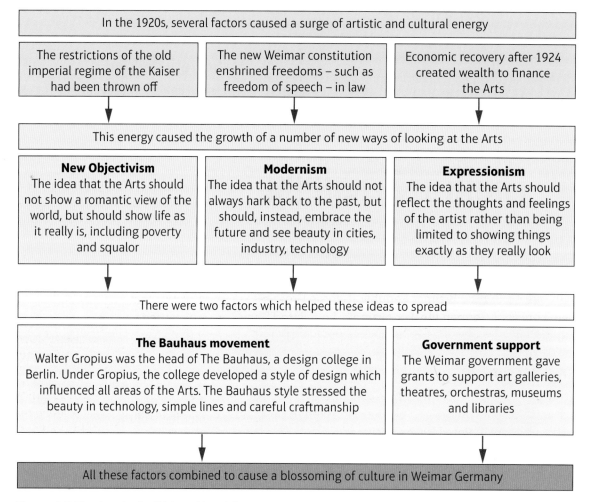

Figure 1.7 The Arts in the Weimar Republic.

Art

In art, painters like **Otto Dix** (see Source B) often painted expressionist versions of scenes from German life which were very critical of German society.

Source C

A poster for *Metropolis* (1926). It shows an artist's view of the wonders of life in the 20th century.

Source B, the painting by Otto Dix, is expressionist in style and shows the harsh life of war veterans and falling standards of behaviour in Germany's night life during the Weimar Republic. George Grosz also painted scenes that were critical of German life. For example, he painted 'Grey Day', which used expressionist images of people to show the boredom of most people's lives.

Architecture

Some architects, like **Erich Mendelsohn**, were influenced by the **Bauhaus** school of design. When Mendelsohn was asked to design the **Einstein Tower**, an observatory in Potsdam, he designed a futuristic tower which looks like a rocket. It was unlike anything seen before.

Cinema

Films became popular all over the world in the 1920s. Some German films were very innovative. *The Cabinet of Dr. Caligari*, for example, was one of the world's first horror films. *Metropolis*, directed by **Fritz Lang** and released in 1926, was a science fiction film about life and technology in the 20th century. It was financed by a government-funded agency called UFA. Germany's first sound film was made in 1930, and by 1932, there were 3,800 German cinemas showing films with sound.

Source B

A painting by Otto Dix, showing a Berlin street scene, from 1927. It is expressionist in style and shows the harsh life of war veterans and falling standards of behaviour in Germany's night life during the Weimar Republic.

Extend your knowledge

First World War literature
Erich Remarque wrote a gritty, realistic anti-war novel called *All Quiet on the Western Front*. Published in 1929, it sold 500,000 copies in three months and was adapted into a film. How was this book similar to work in other areas of the Arts in Germany in the 1920s?

Opposition

Not everyone approved of these extreme changes in the Arts. These changes brought the Weimar Republic under attack from the left and right.

- Those on the left wing, like the KPD, said the funding was money spent on extravagance, when working people needed basic help.
- Those on the right wing, like the nationalists and the Nazi Party, said the changes undermined traditional German culture.

Activities ?

1 Working as a class, point out the elements of Expressionism, Modernism and New Objectivism in Sources B and C and other works of art mentioned on page 37.

2 List reasons why was there so much cultural change in Weimar Germany in the 1920s.

3 Look back at pages 33–38. Write a paragraph to explain the ways that the social changes in the 1920s:

  a helped the Weimar Republic politically

  b harmed the Weimar Republic politically.

Exam-style question, Section B

Study Interpretations 2 and 3 on pages 34 and 36. They give different views about the attitudes towards women in Weimar Germany.

What is the main difference between these views?

Explain your answer, using details from both interpretations. **4 marks**

Exam tip

It is not enough just to find differences of detail between the interpretations. The key is:

- to decide how the view in one interpretation is different from in the other
- to use details in each interpretation to illustrate how the views differ.

Summary

- Some improvements in the standard of living took place. However, they were fragile and helping the working classes was not popular with all Germans in the Weimar Republic.
- There were some improvements in the position of women in politics, at work and in leisure. However, they were limited improvements and they did not please all Germans.
- Dramatic changes occurred in culture, particularly in art, architecture and the cinema. However, these changes did not please all Germans.

Checkpoint

Strengthen

S1 List figures that illustrate changes in unemployment, working hours, wages, housing, the treatment of veterans and higher education.

S2 Give examples of how the position of women improved in politics, work and leisure.

S3 Describe the new ideas in the Arts in Weimar Germany and give examples of how these affected art, architecture and cinema.

Challenge

C1 Give a reasoned view about whether the standard of living went up for most people in Weimar Germany, using specific details to support your answer.

C2 Explain why some people were pleased about changes for women in Weimar Germany, but others were not.

C3 Explain why there was a change in culture in Weimar Germany.

How confident do you feel about your answers to these questions? If you are unsure, look again at page 33 for S1 and C1, pages 34–35 for S2 and C2, pages 36–38 for S3 and C3. If you are still unsure about your answers, join together with others and discuss a joint answer. Your teacher can give you hints.

Recall quiz

1 Who was the first president of the Weimar Republic?

2 Which political party did he belong to?

3 Who replaced him as president in 1925?

4 Who was the minister who dominated Weimar economic and foreign policy from 1923?

5 In what year did he die?

6 The Reichstag was one house of the Weimar parliament. What was the other?

7 What was the minimum age for voting under the Weimar Constitution?

8 What was the title of the Weimar equivalent of the British prime minister?

9 What was Article 48 of the Weimar constitution?

10 What were the initials of the seven main political parties in the Weimar Republic?

Activities ?

1 Make a timeline for 1918 and 1919. On the timeline, mark each of the following events. If possible, give the date, month and year.

   a The abdication of the Kaiser

   b The announcement, by Scheidemann, of the start of the Republic

   c The Council of Representatives take over control of the government

   d The armistice ends the First World War

   e Elections for the National Assembly

   f The National Assembly meets for the first time

   g The Weimar Government signs the Treaty of Versailles

   h The new Weimar constitution is announced

2 Make a list of the reasons Germans hated the Treaty of Versailles. Now shuffle your list into a different order, from the one you think is the most hated at the top to the least hated at the bottom, with a brief reason against each item on the list to explain your decision.

3 Divide a sheet of A4 paper into four. Use the four quarters to list the key events in each of the following episodes:

   a the Spartacist Revolt, 1919

   b the Kapp Putsch, 1920

   c the French occupation of the Ruhr, 1923

   d the struggle against inflation, 1923–24

4 Finish these sentences in as much detail as you can:

   a The Rentenmark was…

   b The Dawes Plan was…

   c The Young Plan was…

   d The Treaty of Locarno was…

   e Joining the League of Nations meant…

   f The Kellogg-Briand Pact was…

5 Give each of the aspects listed below a mark out of 10, to show how much social change it involved. Then write two or three sentences to explain each of your marks.

   a Standards of living

   b The role of women

   c Culture

Writing historically: organising ideas

The most successful historical writing is clearly organised, guiding the reader through the writer's ideas.

Learning outcomes

By the end of this lesson, you will understand how to:

- organise your ideas into paragraphs
- link your paragraphs to guide the reader.

Definitions

Paragraph: a unit of text that focuses on a particular point or idea and information related to it.

How can I organise my ideas into paragraphs?

Look at the notes below written in response to this exam-style question:

Explain why there was opposition in Germany to the Treaty of Versailles (1919). **(12 marks)**

Armistice

Stab in the back — November Criminals

Treaty of Versailles

Diktat

War guilt

Reparations — money had to be paid to allies

Loss military force

Loss total population

Loss of land - colonies

Now look at the full response below.

There were many reasons why Germany opposed the Treaty of Versailles. Firstly, it was seen as a Diktat. Many Germans did not believe they had lost the war, but had been 'stabbed in the back' by the new Weimar government. However, because Germany surrendered, the Treaty of Versailles was a Diktat. This meant that the terms of the treaty were not open to negotiation – as Germany had surrendered, they were not entitled to an opinion. This angered many Germans.

Another reason why Germans opposed the Treaty of Versailles was the 'war guilt' clause. This meant that, since Germany were to blame for the war, they had to pay reparations. This compensation came in many forms. One of the biggest was money: Germany had to repay 136,000 million marks to the Allies. They also had to give away land surrounding Germany, such as Alsace and Lorraine as part of the Treaty of Versailles.

A key part of the 'war guilt' clause was reducing the German military. The Allies believed that this would prevent Germany starting another war. The German army was limited to 100,000 men, the navy was reduced (with no submarines allowed) and Germany were also not allowed an air force. Other countries did not have to do this. Germany were the only country made to reduce their military, which the German people opposed.

1. a. What is the key focus of each of these paragraphs?

b. Why do you think this response chose to focus on these key areas?

c. Why do you think this response chose to sequence these paragraphs in this order?

d. Which points in the notes have not been included in the final response? Why do you think the writer decided not to include them?

2. Look closely at the structure of the first paragraph. Which sentences:

a. clearly indicate the central topic of the paragraph

b. show knowledge and understanding of that topic

c. explain its significance to the question?

02 | Hitler's rise to power, 1919–33

Adolf Hitler was born in Braunau, Austria – not in Germany – on 20 April 1889.

Hitler's early life gave no indication of what was to come. His father was a middle-class Austrian customs official. His mother, to whom he was devoted, died of cancer when he was 18.

Hitler did not excel at school. Though talented at art, he failed to get a place at art academy. Early in his life, he had jobs as a labourer, house painter and even a road sweeper.

In 1913, Hitler moved to Munich, a city in Bavaria in the south of Germany. Soon after, his life was changed by the First World War. He became a solider, and according to his commander, was brave, effective and conscientious. He was wounded twice and awarded the Iron Cross (First Class) for bravery.

The defeat of Germany and the Treaty of Versailles were double blows for Hitler. He later wrote, 'And so, it had all been in vain… and in vain the two million who died… In these nights, hatred grew in me, hatred for those responsible… I, for my part, decided to go into politics.'

Within 15 years, he was Chancellor of Germany.

Learning outcomes

In this chapter, you will learn about:

- the founding of the Nazi Party and its early beliefs, 1920–22
- the Munich Putsch of 1923 and the Nazis' lean years of 1924–28
- the economic depression of 1929 and rapid growth of Nazi support
- how Hitler came to power as Chancellor of Germany, 1932–33.

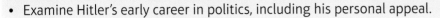

- Examine Hitler's early career in politics, including his personal appeal.
- Understand the policies of the NSDAP.

Hitler's early career in politics

At the end of the First World War, Corporal Adolf Hitler was in hospital in Munich, recovering from gas poisoning. When he was fit enough, the army put him to work keeping an eye on local political activists in the Munich area. As part of this work, Hitler began to attend the meetings of the German Workers' Party (DAP).

Hitler joins the German Worker's Party (DAP)

The DAP had been founded in Munich in February 1919, by Anton Drexler, a railway mechanic. It was tiny – at the first meeting attended by Hitler, on 12 September 1919, there were only 23 people. At the third meeting, the treasurer announced the total party funds as seven marks and 50 pfennigs – enough to buy a few groceries. Even so, Hitler was attracted by the party's ideas and, on 19 September 1919, he joined the DAP.

Setting up the Nazi Party (NSDAP)

Within two years, Hitler had taken control of the DAP and reshaped it into the Nazi Party. There were five parts to this takeover:

- party policy
- Hitler's personal appeal
- party organisation
- party leadership
- the *Sturmabteilung* (SA) or 'Brownshirts'.

Party policy – the Twenty-Five Point Programme

Hitler began to take control of the policies of the DAP. It was a party of protest, strongly opposed to:

- the **Weimar politicians** who deposed the Kaiser, made peace and accepted the Versailles Treaty
- **democracy**, which they believed to be weak, and the Weimar constitution
- the **Jews**, whom they blamed for undermining the German economy.

In January 1920, Hitler became head of party propaganda*. In February, Hitler and Drexler wrote the party's Twenty-Five Point Programme, a document explaining the policies of the DAP (see Source A).

Key term

Propaganda*

A way of controlling public attitudes. Propaganda uses things like newspapers, posters, radio and film, to put ideas into people's minds and therefore shape attitudes.

Source A

Extracts from the Twenty-Five Point Programme, originally produced by the DAP in February 1920.

1 We demand the union of all Germans in a Greater Germany.

2 We demand equality of rights for the German people in its dealings with other nations.

3 We demand land and colonies to feed our people and settle our surplus population.

4 Only those of German blood... are members of the nation. No Jew may be a member of the nation.

7 We demand that the State's primary duty must be to promote work and the livelihood of its citizens.

9 All citizens shall have equal rights and equal duties.

17 We demand... a law to take from the owners any land needed for the common good of the people.

22 We demand... the creation of a people's army.

25 We demand the creation of a strong central state power for the Reich.

Interpretation 1

From *Weimar and Nazi Germany*, by Stephen Lee, in 1996.

The [Twenty-Five Point] programme contained policies which may be described as either nationalist or socialist, or both. The nationalist policies emphasized race, expansion, the army, power and relations with other countries. The socialist policies were to do with state controls over the living conditions of the people and the economy.

Hitler's personal appeal

At first, public support for the DAP depended on popular support for nationalism* and socialism*. However, it quickly became clear that Hitler's personal appeal as an orator (public speaker) was vital in attracting support.

- Hitler rehearsed his speeches carefully. They generally began quietly and slowly, building up the tension towards an impassioned, almost frenzied, rant (see Source B). Although these speeches were frantic rages, they were very persuasive.
- His gestures were a key part of his appeal. At first, he would lean forward and fix his eyes on his audience, drawing them in. Towards the end of his speeches, his hands would wave vigorously in the air.
- He had publicity photos and paintings produced showing him as an orator (see Source C).

Key terms

Nationalism*

A political outlook in which all policies are organised to make the nation stronger and more independent.

Socialism*

A political outlook which stresses that a country's land, industries and wealth should all belong to the workers of that country.

At the 46 party gatherings held between November 1919 and November 1920, Hitler appeared on 31 occasions as the star speaker.

As Hitler's appeal spread, membership of the DAP grew to 1,000 by June 1920 and 3,000 by the end of 1920. Although Hitler was only one of seven on the DAP's organising committee, there was no doubt that the vast majority of new members were Hitler's followers.

Source B

A quotation from a supporter at a Nazi Party meeting in 1926.

A wave of jubilation, rising from afar, moving into the lobby announced the arrival of the Führer [leader]. And then the auditorium went wild. When the speech came to an end… there were tears in my eyes… others, men, women and youngsters were as deeply affected as I.

Activities ?

Consider Source B.

1 What does this quotation tell you about Hitler's place within the DAP?

2 How far can we trust that this view of Hitler was typical of all Germans?

Source C

A painting by Hermann Hoyer. It was exhibited by Adolf Hitler at the Great German Art Exhibition in 1937. It is entitled 'In the beginning there was the word' and shows Hitler addressing a party meeting in 1921.

Party organisation

By 1920, Hitler was Drexler's right-hand man in the DAP. As the party's leader of propaganda, Hitler made his personal mark on the party by introducing a number of changes.

- In January 1920, the DAP set up a permanent office in Munich. Hitler chose Rudolf Schüssler, a friend from the army, as the party's first full-time administrator. The party's meetings were now more organised and better advertised. Party membership and funds began to increase.

- Hitler suggested a new name for the party. The two main pillars of the Twenty-Five Points were nationalism and socialism. Hitler suggested that the party should be called the National Socialist German Workers' Party (NSDAP – or 'Nazi' Party for short). The three parts of the name – national, socialist and workers – all helped to clarify the party policies. It also helped to gain support – Hitler named the party so it appealed to many different people.

- Soon after this, the NSDAP adopted its characteristic logo, the swastika, and its straight-armed party salute. The party was now easy to distinguish from all the other small nationalist parties in German politics.

- By December 1920, the bigger membership and better organisation of the party brought in enough funds for the NSDAP to buy a newspaper – the *Völkischer Beobachter* (the 'People's Observer').

It cost 180,000 marks. Its initial circulation was 11,000 copies, but within a year, it had reached 17,000 copies. The voice of the NSDAP was now widely heard, in Munich, across Bavaria and even across other parts of Germany.

Party leadership

In July 1921, Hitler forced a leadership contest in the party. Drexler was defeated and Hitler became leader of the NSDAP. To consolidate his position, he surrounded himself with supporters to help him lead the party. They were carefully selected for their skills and for the image that they would give the party. They included:

- **Rudolf Hess**, a wealthy academic, who became Hitler's deputy
- **Hermann Goering**, a young, dashing and wealthy First World War fighter pilot
- **Julius Streicher**, a publisher who founded another Nazi newspaper, *Der Stürmer* ('The Stormer')
- **Ernst Röhm**, a scar-faced, bull-necked ex-army officer who was popular amongst ex-soldiers.

Hitler also made powerful friends for the party, such as General Ludendorff, leader of the German Army during the First World War.

Interpretation 2

An extract from *The Weimar Republic,* by John Hiden, published in 1996.

The NSDAP was built up not only on protest but on resentment. This is evident from its programme as well as… the party's chief followers and leading officials. Hitler incorporated in his own person many of the major features on which his movement thrived: the deep sense of frustration, hate against Jews and Marxists (communists)… dislike of parliamentary democracy. To build up a mass movement from such beginnings and keep it together required unique personal qualities. It was clear, for example, from the very beginning that the NSDAP depended heavily on Hitler's spectacular speaking skills.

Extend your knowledge

Julius Streicher (1885–1946)

Julius Streicher joined the Nazi Party in 1922. Like so many other Nazi leaders, he was ex-army and, like Hitler, he had won the Iron Cross. Streicher was already a nationalist politician.

When Streicher brought his supporters into the Nazi Party, it doubled in size overnight. It also extended the geographical appeal of the party. Munich, the NSDAP's headquarters, is in Bavaria, southern Germany. Streicher brought supporters from Franconia, in central Germany.

In 1923, Streicher founded the newspaper, *Der Stürmer*. Its headlines screamed abuse at Jews and communists, and urged those who agreed to join the Nazi Party. It had a circulation of 14,000 copies by 1927.

Make notes to record how important the support of Julius Streicher was to Hitler and the Nazi Party.

The role of the SA (Sturmabteilung)

Sturmabteilung, or stormtroopers, were another way that Hitler kept control of the party. They were formed in August 1921, a month after Hitler took control. The SA was a paramilitary force*. Many of the SA were recruited from the unemployed. They were often ex-soldiers, demobilised from the army, or students. They dressed in brown uniforms and were known as the 'Brownshirts'.

Key term

Paramilitary force*

A private group run like a military force.

The SA paraded in the streets as a show of force. By August 1922, they numbered about 800 and impressed people with a sense of power and organisation. At NSDAP meetings, the SA was used to control the crowds, subduing any opposition to Hitler, often with violence. They were also sent to disrupt opposition meetings. Therefore, the SA strengthened the NSDAP.

Source D

A photograph of the SA on parade, displaying their brown uniforms and the swastika. The flags say, 'Germany awake'.

But the SA also strengthened Hitler. Although Ernst Röhm was put in charge of the SA, Hitler expected them to be completely obedient to him. Many of the SA were wild characters and difficult to control, so Hitler selected trusted members of the SA to be his own personal bodyguard, known as the ***Stosstrupp*** or Shock Troop. Hitler controlled the NSDAP like a military leader.

Hitler gains complete control of the NSDAP

By the party conference of January 1922, Hitler's control of the NSDAP was complete. He persuaded the members to give up their right to elect their leader. There was no discussion of policy at the conference: Hitler dictated policy. His key speech to the party was two and a half hours long. The NSDAP was his party.

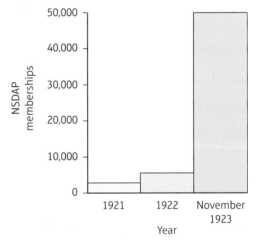

Figure 2.1 Membership figures of the NSDAP.

Interpretation 3

From an article by Gerhard Rempel on Hitler's style of leadership.

The congress was a mile-stone in the organisational history of the NSDAP because it marked the beginning of Hitler's complete, personalised control of the party's… organisational structure… Hitler persuaded the membership to give up voluntarily the rights it had enjoyed under the democratic rules of the NSDAP and to accept instead a framework of discipline and obedience to himself. In turn he promised that his personalised control of the NSDAP would enable the party to play a more effective part in felling [bringing down] the Weimar Republic.

THINKING HISTORICALLY ▶ Interpretations (2b)

The importance of perspective

What we notice when we look at history is shaped by our interests, questions and concepts. Historians are individuals too, and what they 'see' is shaped by what they are interested in and what they see as important. Historians also sometimes use different methods of investigating and will make sense of sources in different ways.

Consider the following question, for example:

How far was the growth of the NSDAP caused by popular support for its policies and how far was it caused by popular support for Hitler, its leader?

	Conceptual approach	Methodology
Historian A	Historian A believes ideas shape history. He believes that powerful feelings, like betrayal and bitterness, can shape what people want and powerful ideas like nationalism and communism can shape what they do.	Historian A looks at the bigger picture. For Weimar Germany, he studies the Versailles peace treaty, economic problems in Germany, examples of political unrest across the country. He sees these national forces controlling events.
Historian B	Historian B thinks people control events. She believes that events are shaped by the choices a nation's people make and by the actions and personality of key individuals, like Hitler.	Historian B uses local sources. She studies what happened to the NSDAP in Munich, the minutes of its meetings, the articles in its newspapers. She reads about Hitler and the opinions of the people who saw Hitler speak.

Answer the following:

  a How would the accounts of Historian A and Historian B differ in response to the question?

  b What factual detail would Historian A use to back up his argument?

  c How would the factual detail used by Historian B differ from this?

  d Do these approaches mean that one account is wrong and the other right? Explain your answer.

  e What does this activity tell you about why interpretations in history differ?

Activities ?

1 Look at pages 43–44. Interpretation 1 says that the key policies of the DAP were nationalism and socialism. Pick out statements from the DAP's Twenty-Five Point Programme in Source A which illustrate i) nationalism and ii) socialism.

2 Discuss with a partner what pages 43–46 tell you about Hitler's personal qualities and how these helped him take control of the NSDAP. Afterwards, write a short summary of your views.

3 Hitler used five strategies to take control of the NSDAP: controlling party policy, personal appeal, controlling party organisation, his leadership takeover and control of the SA.

  a Hold a class debate to decide which one of the five was the most important to allow Hitler to take control of the party.

  b Write a short paragraph on each of the five strategies, and one to explain which was the most important.

Exam-style question, Section A

Give **two** things you can infer from Source A (page 43) about the NSDAP in the 1920s. **4 marks**

Exam tip

This question tests source analysis, specifically the skill of making inferences.

A good answer will suggest something which can be inferred from the source and then quote an extract which shows which part of the source it can be inferred from.

Summary

- Hitler joined the DAP in September 1919.
- Between 1919 and 1923, Hitler took control of the DAP.
- Hitler took over by controlling party policy, using his personal appeal, controlling party organisation, winning the leadership and using the SA.
- Hitler changed the DAP into the NSDAP with distinctive features, such as the swastika, the straight-armed salute and the SA.

Checkpoint

Strengthen

S1 Describe Hitler's first encounters with the DAP.

S2 Describe the policies that Hitler set out for the DAP in the Twenty-Five Point Programme.

S3 Explain Hitler's personal appeal to new party members.

S4 Describe the changes Hitler made to the DAP as he created the NSDAP.

S5 Describe how Hitler created the SA to strengthen himself and the NSDAP.

S6 Describe the growth in membership of the NSDAP, 1920–23.

Challenge

C1 Explain how NSDAP policies appealed to the German people.

C2 Explain how far the growth of the NSDAP was due to its policies and how far was it due to Hitler.

C3 Explain which aspects of Hitler's personal qualities appealed to the German people.

How confident do you feel about your answers to these questions? If you are unsure, look again at pages 43–46 for S1–S6; for C1–C3 you could discuss the answer with other people. Your teacher can provide hints.

The Munich Putsch, 1923

In November 1923, Hitler launched the Munich Putsch*, sometimes called the Beer Hall Putsch. It was an armed revolt intended to overthrow the Weimar Republic. The next few pages will explain the reasons for the revolt, its events and its effects.

Reasons for the Munich Putsch

The Munich Putsch did not occur out of the blue. There was a combination of long-, medium- and short-term causes.

Longer-term causes

From 1918 to 1923, a long list of grievances – such as the 'stab in the back', reparations and the loss of Germany's colonies – had been building up. Amongst some Germans, there was a deep resentment of the Weimar Republic, which created support for nationalist parties like the NSDAP.

From 1919 to 1923, the NSDAP had been growing in its Munich base in Bavaria, south Germany. The Bavarian state government leaders, like Gustav von Kahr, were no fans of the Weimar government. They shared some of the NSDAP's views and turned a blind eye to the violence of the SA. By 1923, the NSDAP had 50,000 members.

Medium-term causes

From 1921 to 1922, Hitler and the NSDAP were heavily influenced by a right-wing party in Italy, called the Fascists, led by Mussolini. They modelled their salute and use of flags on the Fascists. In 1922, Mussolini led his paramilitary forces in a 'march on Rome' forcing the democratic government of Italy to accept him as their new leader.

Short-term causes

During 1923, hyperinflation in Germany reached its peak. Things that cost 100 marks in 1922 cost 200,000 billion marks by 1923. Buying everyday goods became almost impossible. People's savings became useless.

In 1923, French troops entered the German industrial area of the Ruhr and took over German businesses there. When German workers resisted, they were arrested, imprisoned, even deported.

The German people were bitterly aggrieved by these events. The Weimar Republic seemed weak and unable to solve people's problems. The time was ripe to exploit those grievances. In November 1923, Hitler made a bid for power.

Key term

Putsch*
A violent uprising intended to overthrow existing leaders.

Interpretation 1

From *The Coming of the Third Reich*, by Richard J. Evans, published in 2004.

The 'march on Rome' galvanised the fascist movements of Europe… As the situation in Germany began to deteriorate… Hitler began to think that he could do the same in Germany as Mussolini had done in Italy.

Source A

From a report in September 1923 by the Bavarian police.

As a result of rising prices and unemployment, the workers are bitter. The patriotic are at fever pitch because of the failure of the resistance in the Ruhr.

The events of the Munich Putsch

On the evening of 8 November 1923, Bavarian government officials were meeting in a beer hall, called the Burgerbrau Keller, in Munich.

Gustav von Kahr, the leader of the state government of Bavaria, was the main speaker. Others included:

- **von Seisser**, the head of the Bavarian police
- **von Lossow**, the head of the German Army in Bavaria.

Hitler burst in, supported by 600 members of the SA. Brandishing a revolver, he shot into the ceiling and declared that he was taking over the state of Bavaria and would, from there, march on Berlin to overthrow the Weimar Republic. Ludendorff, the famous German general, would become leader of the German Army.

Source B

An announcement made on 9 November 1923 by Gustav von Kahr, leader of the state government of Bavaria.

```
The deception and treachery of ambitious
rebels have changed a peaceful meeting,
held to encourage people to work together,
into a scene of disgusting violence. The
declarations of support, forced from myself,
General von Lossow and Colonel Seisser at
the point of the gun, are null and void. The
National Socialist German Workers' Party
(NSDAP), and the troops who have gathered to
support them, are banned.
```

At gunpoint, Hitler demanded that Kahr, Seisser and Lossow should support him. Overpowered by Hitler and Ludendorff, they reluctantly shook hands in agreement. Meanwhile, Röhm and his SA took over the local police and army headquarters.

Crucially, however, the main army barracks remained in the hands of army officers loyal to the government. When Hitler was elsewhere, Ludendorff released Kahr, Seisser and Lossow. At 5 a.m. the next morning, 9 November, as Hitler and his supporters gathered to launch their attack on the streets of Munich, it became clear that the three Bavarian leaders had withdrawn their support and had decided to put down any uprising.

Hitler hesitated. Eventually, at about midday, he decided to continue with the revolt. He had the support of almost 1,000 SA and they were bolstered by about 2,000 'volunteer' supporters (the SA robbed two local banks, owned by Jews, and paid these supporters with stolen money). Together, Hitler, Ludendorff, Goering, Röhm, Streicher and their followers all marched on the town centre to declare Hitler the President of Germany.

Hitler assumed that there would be support amongst local people and officials. He was to be disappointed.

Source C

A photograph of Hitler's Shock Troop in Munich on the morning of the Putsch, 8 November 1923.

It wasn't just Kahr, Lossow and Seiser who, in the end, failed to support Hitler. Most of the townspeople remained indifferent and the army stayed loyal to the state government. Hitler, with only 2,000 rifles, was outgunned.

Hitler and Ludendorff, both ex-soldiers, led a group of Hitler's Shock Troop to the main square, where they were met by state police. According to police reports, the rebels pressed pistols into the policemen's chests, spat on them and pointed bayonets in their direction. Then someone – it is not clear which side – opened fire.

A bodyguard, Graf, threw himself in front of Hitler and was wounded by half a dozen bullets. Goering was shot in the thigh. Hitler was dragged to the ground by his bodyguards, with such force that his left arm was dislocated. In moments, 14 of Hitler's supporters and four policemen were shot dead.

Source D

A painting from 1940 by H. Schmitt, one of Hitler's followers, who took part in the Munich Putsch. Hitler stands at the front of the rebels with his arm raised, with Ludendorff on his right.

At this point, the rebellion descended into chaos.

- Most of the rebels scrambled for refuge; one group entered a school for girls and hid under a bed.
- Ludendorff, Röhm and Streicher were all arrested. Goering was spirited away by supporters and went into hiding abroad.
- Hitler fled the scene in a car, then hid at the house of a friend, Ernst Hanfstaengl, ten miles south of Munich. He was later found, hiding in a wardrobe, and arrested on 11 November.

Interpretation 2

From *Adolf Hitler* by John Tolund, published in 1996.

The state police rounded up hundreds [of rebels], disarming them on the street. The rebels left behind at the beer hall to hold the command post were so unstrung [unsettled] by the catastrophe that they surrendered without resistance to police. They stacked up their arms and went home to brood. The Putsch was over. But victorious state police marching away from the beer hall were abused by indignant citizens, with cries of "Betrayers of the Fatherland! Jew defenders! Bloodhounds! Heil Hitler – Down with Kahr!"

Activity ?

What does Interpretation 2 tell you about:

a the armed rebels who supported Hitler

b support for the revolt in the general population of Munich?

Activities ?

1 Hold a class debate about whether the occupation of the Ruhr was the key reason for the Munich Putsch. Afterwards, record what you believe caused the Munich Putsch.

2 Draw a timeline covering 8 to 11 November 1923. Mark on it the key events of the Munich Putsch.

3 Look at Source D on page 51.

   a What impression does it give you about Hitler's part in the Munich Putsch?

   b How is it different from what you know about the Munich Putsch?

   c How would you account for the differences?

4 Look at Source E opposite. What does it tell you about the part played by the key leaders of the Bavarian authorities in the Munich Putsch?

Source E

A 1924 cartoon from the political magazine *Simplicissimus*. Hitler is shown setting fire to the town. He is being carried by von Lossow, the head of the German Army in Bavaria, and von Kahr, the leader of the state government of Bavaria. Meanwhile, Kahr shouts out: 'Officer, arrest that arsonist up there.'

Exam-style question, Section A

Explain why the Munich Putsch (1923) failed.

You may use the following in your answer:

- the German army
- Bavarian leaders.

You **must** also use information of your own. **12 marks**

Exam tip

A good answer will:

- include several factors that were reasons for failure
- contain detailed information about each factor and how it weakened the revolt.

THINKING HISTORICALLY Interpretations (4a)

The weight of evidence

Historians' interpretations are not simply their opinions. Interpretations are theories. In order for theories to be strong, they need to be backed up with convincing evidence. When you evaluate an interpretation, you should consider how strong the evidence is for the conclusions it comes to.

When you write your own interpretations of historical events, you too should be using evidence to make your conclusions as strong as possible.

Below, there are three 'Conclusions' that students have written about Hitler's reasons for the Munich Putsch. They are based on Source F.

Work in pairs. Read Source F and the three conclusions below, then answer the questions.

Conclusion 1

Hitler planned the Munich Putsch because he wanted power for himself. This is clear because he says, 'the national government will be taken over by me'.

Conclusion 2

Hitler planned the Munich Putsch because he wanted a stronger Germany. We know this because he said he would replace the 'wretched Germany of today' with a Germany of 'greatness, freedom and splendour. Further evidence is that Hitler's first appointments are the leaders of the armed forces, the army, the police; this shows he wanted a strong Germany. Finally, Hitler saying that the Bavarian prime minister would have dictatorial powers shows that he wanted a strong Germany.

Conclusion 3

Hitler planned the Munich Putsch because he wanted right-wing government in Germany. He proposed a Regent, or temporary monarch in Bavaria. He also proposed a Bavarian prime minister with dictatorial powers.

1 Write out each conclusion and then use highlighter pens to colour code them. Use one colour for 'evidence', another colour for 'conclusions' and a third for language that shows 'reasoning' (e.g. "therefore", "so").

2 How do the conclusions differ in terms of the way that the evidence is used?

3 Put the conclusions in ranking order from the best to the worst. Explain your choice.

4 Consider what you know about the Munich Putsch. For each conclusion, add any extra evidence you can think of that supports that conclusion.

5 Rank the conclusions again. Does the evidence you've added change which you think is the best?

6 Using evidence from the source and your own knowledge, write your own conclusion about the level of support Hitler had during the putsch. Remember to back up all your points by reasoning about the evidence.

Source F

An extract from a speech made by Adolf Hitler at the Bergerbrau Keller on the evening of 8 November 1923.

The Bavarian government is removed. I propose that a new Bavarian government shall be formed consisting of a Regent [a temporary monarch] and a Prime Minister who will have dictatorial powers. I propose Herr von Kahr as Regent and Herr Pohner as Prime Minister.

The national government of the November Criminals and the Reich President in Berlin are declared to be removed. I propose that, until we can bring the November criminals to account, the national government will be taken over by me. Ludendorff will take over the leadership of the German National Army, Lossow will be German Minister for the Armed Forces, Seisser will be the German Police Minister.

I want now to fulfil the vow which I made to myself five years ago when I was a blind cripple in the military hospital: to know neither rest nor peace until the November criminals had been overthrown, until on the ruins of the wretched Germany of today there should have arisen once more a Germany of power and greatness, freedom and splendour.

Interpretation 3

From *The Coming of the Third Reich*, by Richard J. Evans, published in 2004.

It seems likely that they (the Bavarian authorities) offered Hitler leniency in return for his agreement to carry the can [take responsibility]. As judge, they picked... a well-known nationalist... Hitler was allowed to wear his Iron Cross and address the court for hours on end... The court grounded its leniency in the fact that the participants *'were led in their action by pure patriotic spirit and noble will'*. The judgement was scandalous even by the standards of the Weimar judiciary.

Source G

From a letter, written by Hitler in 1924, while in prison after the Munich Putsch.

When I resume active work, it will be necessary to pursue a new policy. Instead of working to achieve power by an armed coup, we will have to hold our noses and enter the Reichstag. If outvoting them takes longer than outshooting them, at least the result will be guaranteed by their own constitution. Sooner or later we shall have a majority, and after that – Germany!

Consequences of the Munich Putsch

Hitler and several other leaders of the Putsch were put on trial.

- Ludendorff was found not guilty – more by the support of the judge than the evidence.
- Hitler and three others were found guilty of treason and sentenced to five years in Landsberg Prison.
- The NSDAP was banned.

In the short term, the Munich Putsch was therefore a defeat and a humiliation for Hitler. Hitler was released after only nine months. This leniency was not uncommon. However, in the longer term, the results were not all bad for him.

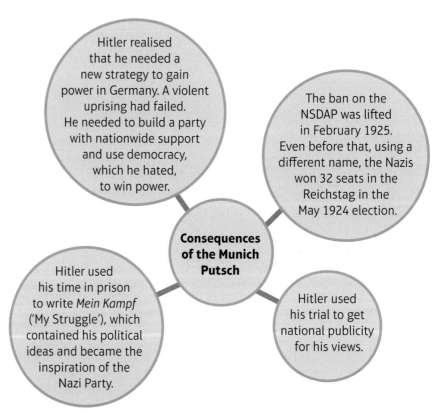

Figure 2.2 Consequences of the Munich Putsch.

Activities ?

1 Consider the results of the Munich Putsch.

  a Make a list of the ways in which it might be considered a failure for Hitler and the Nazi Party.

  b Now make a list of the ways it might be considered a success.

  c Draw a set of weighing scales. On one side, write the ways the Munich Putsch was a failure and, on the other side, the ways it was a success.

  d Make a judgement: overall, was the Munich Putsch a failure or a success? Write a paragraph to justify your judgement.

The lean years of the Nazi Party, 1924–28

Mein Kampf

Hitler read widely during his time in Landsberg Prison. He later described this as 'a free education at the state's expense'. Many of the ideas he read were recorded in *Mein Kampf*, which he wrote whilst in prison. Much of it was dictated and written out by a fellow Nazi, Rudolf Hess, who later became deputy leader of the party.

Mein Kampf is a key source of information about the political beliefs of Hitler's Nazi Party after 1924. For example, *Mein Kampf* makes Hitler's extreme racist views very clear.

- Hitler believed that the German race (which he called the **Aryan race**) was destined to rule the world.
- But he said that there was a Jewish conspiracy to undermine Aryan rule.
- Jews, he said, planned to weaken the Aryan race by intermarriage, and by taking over German industry and the moderate political groups such as the Social Democrat Party.

Hitler's other views, expressed in *Mein Kampf*, were familiar from the early days of the NSDAP.

- **Nationalism** – reviving the power of Germany, for example by reversing the Versailles Treaty. By this time, Hitler was also stressing the need for *Lebensraum* (living space) for the German people to expand into. He openly spoke of the need for Germany to invade Russian land to the east of Germany, to drive out the communists and provide land for German farmers to produce food to feed the German nation.
- **Socialism** – using the wealth of industry and land to benefit German working people, not rich landowners and industrialists.
- **Totalitarianism** – throwing off democracy, which Hitler believed was weak, and instead putting power in the hands of the state – preferably one leader who could organise everything for the benefit of the people.

- **Traditional German values** – such as strong family values, clear male and female roles, a strong work ethic, Christian morality and old-style German art, music and theatre.

Source H

A NSDAP campaign poster from 1924. It emphasises Nazi principles of family, work and nationalism.

Party reorganisation, 1924–28

Hitler was soon able to resume his political career and take the views written in *Mein Kampf* to the German electorate.

- He was released from prison on 20 December 1924, after just nine months of his five-year sentence.
- The ban on the NSDAP was lifted on 16 February 1925.
- Hitler was able to relaunch the NSDAP at a meeting in Munich on 27 February that year.
- The lenient treatment of Hitler and the Nazi Party were typical of the way the law courts treated violent right-wing attacks on the Weimar Republic (see page 22 for comparison).

However, the failure of the Munich Putsch had persuaded Hitler that he could not rely on violence to take control of Germany. He had to be elected to power. He therefore made the Nazis a much better-organised political party.

Nazi Party headquarters

The central hub of the Nazi Party was at its party headquarters, based in Munich.

- Philipp Bouhler was appointed party secretary and Franz Schwarz was appointed party treasurer. They made sure that the Nazi party was well organised and well financed.
- The party was organised like a mini state, with Hitler as the leader and departments for all aspects of government, such as finance, foreign affairs, industry, agriculture and education.
- As well as its paramilitary arm, the SA, the party also had a women's section called The German Women's Order. For younger people, a National Socialist German Students' League was created – the Hitler Youth for 14- to 18-year-olds, alongside a School Pupils' League.

The creation of a national Nazi Party

The rest of Germany was divided into 35 regions or *Gaue*, one for each constituency of the Weimar Republic. Each *Gau* had a leader, or *Gauleiter*, the local leader of the Nazi Party. *Gauleiters* were rarely appointed. Hitler relied on the most able leaders forcing their way to the top, rather like he had done in the DAP.

- **Gregor Strasser** became a powerful *Gauleiter* in the north of Germany.
- **Joseph Goebbels** rose to prominence in the Rhineland.

To pay for all this, Hitler overhauled party finances. He raised money from wealthy industrialists who shared some of Hitler's nationalist views and also hoped that he would be powerful enough to control the trade unions. Eventually, the Nazi Party received loans from big businessmen, like Thyssen, Krupp and Bosch.

The Schutzstaffel or SS

Hitler also strengthened the paramilitary forces of the Nazi Party. By 1930, he had expanded the SA to 400,000 members. However, the Munich Putsch had taught Hitler the importance of a totally loyal group of bodyguards – and he didn't trust the SA.

- Many stormtroopers were violent thugs and difficult to control.
- While Hitler was in prison, the SA had become loyal to Ernst Röhm, its commander.

So, in 1925, Hitler took two steps to tighten his control of his paramilitary forces.

- First, he replaced Röhm as leader of the SA. Röhm was forced to find work abroad until he returned to the Nazi Party in 1930.
- Then he set up a new party security group. He called them the *Schutzstaffel* ('Protection Squad'), or SS. It was a smaller group, with specially selected members, so that they could be trusted to act as Hitler's personal bodyguard.

At first, the SS was run by Hitler's personal chauffeur and bodyguard, Julius Schreck. However, soon after, Hitler placed them under the control of Heinrich Himmler, a more senior member of the Nazi Party. Himmler expanded the SS to 3,000 members by 1930. They were famous – and feared – for their menacing black uniforms, which were introduced in 1932.

Source I

A photograph of a parade of SS members in Nuremberg in 1933.

The Bamberg Conference of 1926

By early 1926, it was clear that the local power of *Gauleiters* was creating a split in the Nazi Party.

- Some party activists, such as Strasser and Goebbels, were based in northern, urban and industrial areas, like Berlin and the Ruhr. They emphasised the **socialist** part of National Socialism. They stressed benefits for workers and attacks on businessmen and landowners.
- But other party leaders, such as Hitler himself, were in southern, more rural areas of Germany, like Bavaria, the heartland of the Nazi Party. They emphasised the **nationalist** part of National Socialism. They stressed a strong German state and action against the Jews.

Hitler called a national conference of the Nazi Party to address this split. He based it in Bamberg, in Bavaria. Partly because of the location, southern party leaders made up the majority of the conference.

- Northern leaders, like Strasser, were allowed to put their views forward.
- But Hitler made his own views clear. He spoke for five hours. He made it seem that the 'socialist' wing of the party were more like communists – the enemies of the Nazis.
- Hitler also made great efforts to win Goebbels over to his side. As a result, Goebbels abandoned Strasser's arguments, much to Strasser's disgust. Strasser called Goebbels 'a scheming dwarf'.

The Bamburg Conference therefore had a big impact on the Nazi Party.

- Hitler's control of the party was now clear. Goebbels was promoted to *Gauleiter* of Berlin as a reward. Strasser pledged his loyalty to Hitler, but Hitler never really trusted him. Strasser was murdered in 1934, during a clear-out of Nazi leaders (see page 80).
- The 'socialist' principles of the Nazi Party were weakened. This gave Hitler more freedom to adopt any policies he liked.

Reasons for limited support, 1923–29

By 1929, the Nazi Party was well organised. It had 100,000 members and Hitler had tightened his personal control over the party. However, in some ways, these were lean years. There were several reasons for this.

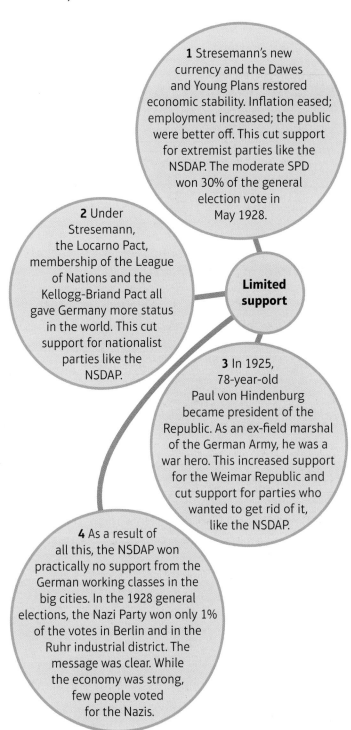

1 Stresemann's new currency and the Dawes and Young Plans restored economic stability. Inflation eased; employment increased; the public were better off. This cut support for extremist parties like the NSDAP. The moderate SPD won 30% of the general election vote in May 1928.

2 Under Stresemann, the Locarno Pact, membership of the League of Nations and the Kellogg-Briand Pact all gave Germany more status in the world. This cut support for nationalist parties like the NSDAP.

Limited support

3 In 1925, 78-year-old Paul von Hindenburg became president of the Republic. As an ex-field marshal of the German Army, he was a war hero. This increased support for the Weimar Republic and cut support for parties who wanted to get rid of it, like the NSDAP.

4 As a result of all this, the NSDAP won practically no support from the German working classes in the big cities. In the 1928 general elections, the Nazi Party won only 1% of the votes in Berlin and in the Ruhr industrial district. The message was clear. While the economy was strong, few people voted for the Nazis.

Figure 2.3 Reasons for limited Nazi support, 1923–29.

Source J

A confidential report on the Nazis by the Interior Ministry, July 1927.

```
A numerically insignificant... radical-
revolutionary splinter group incapable of
exerting any noticeable influence on the
great mass of the people and the course of
political events.
```

As a result, moderate parties did well between 1924 and 1928, and all the extreme parties lost ground. In the general elections of May 1928, the Nazis:

- won only 12 seats
- were only the seventh biggest Reichstag party
- polled only 810,000 votes – just 2.6% of the total vote.

Activities ?

1 Did Hitler's reorganisation of the Nazi Party after 1924 make the party more effective, or did it just increase Hitler's control of the party? Debate this in a group, then write your own opinion.

2 List the reasons why, despite all Hitler's work, the Nazis were still relatively weak in 1928.

a Make sure that you can give some details for each reason.

b Identify which of these was the main reason and explain your choice.

Summary

- Hitler launched the Munich Putsch in November 1923, in an attempt to take control of Germany.
- The Munich Putsch failed, but in some ways Hitler and the Nazis benefitted.
- Hitler relaunched the Nazi Party in 1925, having set out his ideas in *Mein Kampf*.
- Hitler reformed the central and national organisation of the Nazi Party.
- Hitler strengthened his control over the party and over the SA.
- By 1928, the Nazis had little influence in the Reichstag.

Checkpoint

Strengthen

S1 Describe the events of the Munich Putsch and Hitler's trial.

S2 Explain Hitler's political views, as expressed in *Mein Kampf*.

S3 Describe how Hitler improved the central and national organisation of his party.

S4 Give details of how strong the Nazi Party was by 1928.

Challenge

C1 Why did Hitler launch the Munich Putsch in 1923?

C2 Why did the Munich Putsch fail?

C3 How far, and with what effect, did the organisation of the Nazi Party improve, 1924–28?

How confident do you feel about your answers to these questions? If you are unsure, look again at pages 49–57 for S1–S4; for C1–C3, you could join together with others and discuss a joint answer. Your teacher can provide hints.

Why, in just a few months, did the confidence in the Weimar Republic disappear?

- Confidence started to ebb away on 3 October 1929, when Stresemann had a heart attack and died. The loss of his expertise was a severe blow to the Weimar Republic.
- Then things became worse. Later in October 1929, there was a world economic crisis, known as the Great Depression. In Germany, it caused economic collapse, widespread unemployment and a political crisis.

The Wall Street Crash in the USA

In October 1929, share prices began to fall on the Wall Street stock exchange in New York, USA.

- Falling shares meant people's investments fell in value.
- Worried about losing money, people rushed to sell shares before the fell further.
- On 'Black Thursday', 24 October 1929, 13 million shares were sold. This panic selling sent prices even lower. Shares worth $20,000 in the morning were worth $1,000 by the end of the day's trading.
- Within a week, investors had lost $4,000 million.

This event is known as the Wall Street Crash.

Economic effects in Germany

The first effect of the Wall Street Crash on Germany was that it caused a banking crisis. German banks were major investors in shares on the US stock exchange and suffered huge losses. German banks lost so much money that German people feared they wouldn't have access to the money in their bank accounts.

People rushed to queue up outside the banks and get their money out – causing some German banks to run out of cash. The German Civil Servant bank, for example, went bust in 1929, meaning many people lost their savings.

The collapse of German banking then caused a general economic collapse in German industry. This was because, to pay out the money demanded by their account holders, German and American banks urgently needed cash. These banks began to demand the return of money they had lent to businesses in industry and agriculture. Deprived of this money, German industries and farms had to cut back production or even close down completely. The economy collapsed.

Source A

A photograph of people crowding outside the locked doors of the German Civil Servant Bank in 1929, demanding their money back.

Unemployment

The banking crisis and the subsequent economic collapse in Germany was disastrous for employment.

- When the banks demanded their money back from German industries and farms, they had to scale back production or close. Either way, they made workers unemployed.

- The economic crisis was worldwide. German companies that sold their goods abroad found that their sales fell. They had to make even more workers unemployed.

- German workers who were unemployed became poorer. They couldn't afford to buy as much. This meant that sales fell even further and companies had to make even more workers unemployed. It was a downward spiral for German industry.

The tables below show the downward spiral of German industry.

	Fall in industrial output
1929–30	10% fall
1929–31	30% fall
1929–32	40% fall

Date	Unemployment
September 1929	1.3 million
September 1931	4.3 million
September 1932	5.1 million
January 1933	6.1 million

Unemployment – the impact on people

By January 1933, six million workers were unemployed. This included 40% of all factory workers, 50% of all Germans between 16 and 30 years old, and 60% of university graduates. As a result, many types of people suffered.

- **Unemployed**. As the number of people out of work grew, the government became unable to pay unemployment benefits. Taxes were raised and unemployment benefits were cut, causing even bigger problems for the unemployed.

- **Savers**. Some people had their savings invested in shares. When share prices crashed in 1929, the value of their savings crashed too. This meant, if they became unemployed, they had no savings to fall back on.

- **Workers**. Those in work suffered too. As mentioned above, their taxes went up. But, worse still, with people desperate for work, employers cut wages. Real wages* in 1932 were 70% of 1928 levels.

- **Homeless**. Many people could no longer afford their rent and became homeless. Shanty towns of makeshift houses began to spring up, and the unemployed wandered the streets looking for work or food. Boredom turned to violence. After a while, fights broke out in the streets between police and roaming bands of young men. There was an increase of 24% in arrests for theft in Berlin. The German people were desperate.

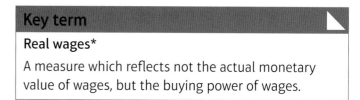

Key term

Real wages*

A measure which reflects not the actual monetary value of wages, but the buying power of wages.

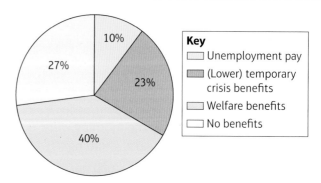

Key
- ☐ Unemployment pay
- ▨ (Lower) temporary crisis benefits
- ☐ Welfare benefits
- ☐ No benefits

Figure 2.4 Government financial support for the unemployed in 1932. Unemployment totalled six million people.

Activities

1. Draw a spider diagram to show the connection between the following: the Wall Street Crash, banking crisis, company closures, unemployment, falling wages, rising taxes, falling benefits. Write a statement to explain what the diagram shows.

2. Write a paragraph to explain how **economic** collapse (1929–32) led to **political** collapse.

3. Explain why support for the Communist Party rose, 1929–32.

The failure to deal with unemployment

People demanded political action, but the Weimar government failed them. From 1930 to 1932, the chancellor was Heinrich Brüning, leader of the Centre Party. First, he proposed higher taxes to pay for unemployment benefit. Then he put fixed time limits on unemployment benefits, to make payments more affordable.

This pleased no one. Right-wing parties, the middle classes and the wealthy opposed higher taxes. Left-wing parties and the working classes opposed reduced benefits. Crucially, the leader of the moderate Social Democrat Party, Hermann Muller, refused to support Brüning's policies. In July 1930, the policies were rejected in the Reichstag by 256 votes to 193. This failure by the moderate parties to work together made the Reichstag powerless to make policy. Whereas the Reichstag met 94 times in 1930, it met only 41 times in 1931 and only 13 times in 1932.

Unable to get laws passed in the Reichstag, Brüning could only govern by decree; he used Article 48 in the constitution to ask the president to pass emergency laws. There had only been five presidential decrees in 1930. As the crisis deepened, Brüning's government had to rely on 44 decrees in 1931 and 66 in 1932.

But even this was in vain – the causes of suffering were beyond government control, so the suffering continued. Useless decrees merely undermined confidence in the Weimar Republic still further.

Brüning had lost control of the Reichstag, the economy and the streets. He resigned in May 1932.

Rise in support for KPD and NSDAP

As life became harder, and moderate parties failed to solve Germany's economic problems, people abandoned the moderates and – as the table   shows – switched to extremist parties such as the Nazis and the Communist Party (KPD).

General elections, 1928–32: seats in the Reichstag			
	May 1928	Sept 1930	July 1932
Social Democrats (SPD)	152	143	133
Nazi Party (NSDAP)	12	107	230
Communists (KPD)	54	77	89

Growing support for the Communist Party (KPD)

As Germany's social and economic problems increased during the Great Depression, support for the German Communist Party (KPD) grew. Whereas 10% of voters supported the KPD in the Reichstag elections of 1928, 15% of voters supported them in 1932. This represented over a million extra voters. By 1932, the KPD was the largest communist party in the world, outside the Soviet Union.

Support for the KPD was especially strong amongst the working class in large towns, for two reasons:

1 **Growing unemployment** – which reached five million in 1932
2 **Falling wages** – real wages in 1932 were about 15% lower than in 1928.

Many working-class people saw the communists as the only party who would defend their jobs and their wages against employers and landowners.

However, as the table above shows, support for the Nazi Party grew faster than support for the communists. This was partly because the idea of a communist government scared the German middle and upper classes. They feared that they would suffer under a communist government and that they might have their land and their companies confiscated by the state.

As communist support grew, the middle and upper classes therefore became even more likely to vote for the NSDAP, because they saw Hitler as their best defence against the communists. Fear of communism became another reason for the rise in support for the Nazi Party.

Why did people support the Nazi Party?

The growth in support for the Nazis from 1929 to 1933 was spectacular. Why did it happen?

The appeal of Hitler and the SA

Many Germans were fed up with the Weimar Republic. They thought its government was weak, that it was bullied by other nations and that it had failed to solve economic problems. They saw Hitler and the Nazis as an alternative.

In Hitler, they saw a strong leader who promised:

- to restore law and order
- to force other countries to scrap the Treaty of Versailles and treat Germany fairly.

Hitler was very popular. He featured prominently in Nazi posters and spoke in as many parts of the country as possible. He also took advantage of new approaches to electoral campaigning. For example, he used aeroplanes in a whirlwind campaign for the 1930 and 1932 elections. The Nazis had support from wealthy businessmen (see page 56). This provided them with vital funding for the costs of running an election campaign, such as posters, radio broadcasts and aeroplanes.

The SA was another reason why Germans supported the Nazi Party.

- The uniformed SA made the Nazis seem organised, disciplined and reliable. During economic and social turmoil, the SA made the Nazis look strong enough to control unrest and stand up to foreign powers.
- The SA were also used to disrupt opposition parties. The Nazis had a stronger private army than the communists. By 1930, the SA had 400,000 stormtroopers. In contrast, the KPD's Red Front Fighters had only about 130,000. The elections of 1930 and 1932 were violent. Armed and uniformed SA tore down the opposition's posters, intimidated their candidates, broke into their offices and disrupted their rallies. In 1932, in one clash with communists near Hamburg, 18 people were killed.

The appeal of the Nazis to different sections of German society

The Nazis also had particular policies that appealed to particular sections of German society (Interpretation 1).

Big business

The leaders of big businesses were one group targeted by the Nazi Party. Wealthy industrialists usually supported the National Party. But this party, along with other moderate parties, had been powerless to solve Germany's economic problems between 1929 and 1933. Hitler persuaded wealthy businessmen that the Nazi Party was their best hope of protection from the rise of the communists.

Source B

From an interview with a member of the Nazi Party.

... for five years I remained unemployed and I was broken both in body and spirit and I learned how stupid were all my dreams in those hard days at university. I was not wanted by Germany... then I was introduced to Hitler. You won't understand and I cannot explain either because I don't know what happened, but life for me took on a tremendous new significance... I committed myself, body, soul and spirit, to the movement.

Interpretation 1

From *The Coming of the Third Reich*, by Richard J. Evans, published in 2004.

... Nazi propaganda... skilfully targeted specific groups in the German electorate... providing topics for particular venues and picking the speaker to fit the occasion. The... Party recognised the growing divisions of German society into competing interest groups in the course of the Depression and tailored their message to their particular constituency. The Nazis adapted... a whole range of posters and leaflets designed to win over different parts of the electorate.

As a result, Nazi finances benefitted. Wealthy businessmen, like Benz and Krupps, poured money into the NSDAP. Nazi propaganda benefitted too. The National Party leader, Alfred Hugenberg, was a newspaper tycoon. He allowed Goebbels to use his newspapers for Nazi propaganda against the communists.

Working-class support

The NSDAP also tried to seem like the party of the German working classes. Their name, the National Socialist German Workers' Party, was an obvious sign of this. They also had policies that appealed to workers. For example, the Nazis supported traditional German values and aimed to create a stronger Germany. To attract working-class voters, the Nazis also promised people 'Work and Bread' on their posters.

However, more workers preferred the communists. Although many working-class people voted for the Nazis, they never dominated the working-class vote (Interpretation 2).

Middle-class support

Another key group in the growth of Nazi support was the middle class, which contained professional people such as teachers and lawyers, business people and small farmers (see Interpretation 2). They often owned land or businesses and had savings. Between 1929 and 1932, they deserted the more moderate parties and many switched their support to the Nazis. There were several reasons for this.

- The Great Depression had hurt the middle classes. Many had lost their companies, their savings or their pensions. They saw Hitler as a strong leader who could help the country recover.
- After 1929, they were also afraid of the growing Communist Party. The communists wanted to abolish private ownership of land and businesses. The middle classes saw the Nazis as a strong party that could protect them from the communists.
- Many middle-class people believed that there had been a moral decline under the Weimar Republic, with more drinking and sexual openness. They saw the Nazis as a return to traditional German values.

Farmers

The Nazis also targeted support from farmers. In 1928, the Nazi policy of confiscating all private land (in the Twenty-Five Points of 1920) was changed. The new policy said that private land would only be confiscated if it was owned by Jews. This reassured farmers. They hoped that Hitler would protect them from the Communist Party, which would have confiscated their land.

This meant that farmers were a strong section of support for the Nazi Party. In the 1930 Reichstag elections, the Nazis gained 60% of the votes in some rural areas.

Young people

The Nazis also targeted support from young Germans. For many young people, the Nazi Party was exciting. Its rallies were colourful and full of atmosphere. Hitler's speeches were stirring and promised more than the traditional parties. Hitler attracted many younger people to become members (see Interpretation 2).

Interpretation 2

From *The Weimar Republic*, by John Hiden, published in 1996.

More than any other party, the NSDAP depended on the crisis for its successful growth. The official membership statistics show an increase from 129,000 to 849,000 from 1930 to 1933…

No fewer than 43% of new members entering the party… were aged 18–30…

The preponderance [number] of petit-bourgeoisie [lower middle class] was particularly striking. White-collar workers, artisans, merchants, shopkeepers and civil servants were twice as strongly represented in the NSDAP than in society as a whole. Manual workers were under-represented (but) of the 270,000 workers who did join the party, 150,000 were unemployed.

Women

At first, many women did not support the Nazis. The Nazi Party argued that women should play a traditional role in society as wives and mothers. Nazi propaganda made special appeals to women. It claimed that voting for the NSDAP was best for their country and best for their families. Increasingly, many women came to see this as attractive.

Unity – something for everyone

In one sense, the Nazis targeted support from specific sections of society. However, in another sense, the Nazi appeal was not to groups, but to the **whole nation** (see Source D). Some historians say this was new for German politics and helped the NSDAP to grow, as shown in Interpretation 3.

Source C

A Nazi Party poster from 1932, appealing to women to support Adolf Hitler for the sake of their family.

Source D

Hitler's speech to the people of Germany on the day of his appointment as Chancellor of Germany on 31 January 1933.

We do not recognise classes. The German people, with its millions of farmers, citizens and workers, will, together, overcome distress.

Interpretation 3

From *Adolf Hitler*, by John Toland, published in 1976.

In 1930, he was offering something new to Germans – unity. He welcomed all. There was no class distinction; the only demand was to follow him in his fight against Jews and Reds, in his struggle for Lebensraum and the glory and good of Germany.

Activities ?

1 What evidence is there on pages 61–64 that the Nazi Party grew in popularity, 1929–33?

2 Divide your class into groups representing big business, farmers, the working class, the middle class, young Germans and women. Each group should try to argue that it was the most important group in the rise of the Nazi Party, 1929–33.

   a Write a paragraph arguing which group you think was most important, and why.

   b Write a paragraph arguing which group you think was least important, and why.

3 'Hitler was the main reason for the rise in support for the Nazi Party, 1929–33'. Write a list of reasons for and against this statement.

THINKING HISTORICALLY Interpretations (2c/3a)

History as hypotheses

In science, you might have come across the idea of a hypothesis – a hypothesis is an idea that a scientist comes up with to explain what they can see happening. The scientist then tries to find evidence, through experiments, to find out whether their hypothesis is correct. Historians often work in a similar way, but look at sources to find their evidence, rather than doing experiments.

These three historians are thinking about the reasons for the rise of the Nazi Party.

Historian's interests	Historian's hypothesis	Evidence
Political historian: Interested in relationships between nations and political leaders, their views and actions and the effects these had on history.		
Economic historian: Interested in how economic conditions changed, and how this affected individual groups in society and their political views.		
Cultural historian: Interested in the ideas in society, how these ideas change and how these ideas affect what people do.	The main reasons for the rise of the Nazi Party were ideas like nationalism, militarism and anti-Semitism. Hitler used these to come to power.	

Work in groups of three.

1 Make a copy of the above table.

   a As a group, discuss the interests of each historian and write a hypothesis that they might put forward based on their interests (the cultural historian has been done for you).

   b Each person in the group should take on the role of one of the historians. For your historian, add at least three pieces of evidence into the table that support your hypothesis, based on the information and sources in this chapter.

   c For your historian, write a final paragraph, summing up your views on the reasons for the rise of the Nazi Party. Remember to restate your hypothesis and support it with evidence.

2 Share your concluding paragraphs with the rest of the group and compare them.

   a Underline instances where different hypotheses use the same or similar evidence.

   b Look at each hypothesis in turn. Can you think of at least one piece of evidence that challenges each hypothesis? (Tip: you can start by looking at evidence for the other hypotheses being right!)

3 Discuss as a group: Is it possible to say which hypothesis is correct?

Exam-style question, Section B

Study Interpretation 1 (page 62) and Interpretation 3 (page 64). They give different views about the reasons for the appeal of the Nazi Party to the German people, 1929–33.

What is the main difference between these views?

Explain your answer, using details from both interpretations.   **4 marks**

Exam tip

It is not enough just to find differences of detail between the interpretations.

The key is:

• to decide how the **view** in one interpretation is different from the other

• **use the detail** in each interpretation to illustrate how the views differ.

Summary

• By the start of 1929, the Nazi Party had little political power in Germany.

• However, by 1932, they had 230 seats in the German Reichstag.

• A key factor was the economic crisis caused by the Wall Street Crash.

• The economic crisis included a banking collapse, a fall in industrial output, rising unemployment and falling wages.

• The Weimar government failed to solve these problems.

• As a result, support grew for extremist parties like the Communist Party and the Nazi Party.

• Support for the Nazis came from several different sections of German society.

Checkpoint

Strengthen

S1 Describe the events of the Wall Street Crash.

S2 Explain the impact of the Wall Street Crash on Germany.

S3 Describe how the German chancellor, Brüning, tried to solve the economic crisis.

S4 Detail the effect of the economic crisis on support for the Communist Party.

S5 Detail the effect of the economic crisis on support for the Nazi Party.

S6 Describe which sections of German society supported the Nazi Party.

Challenge

C1 Explain which aspect of the economic crisis was most important in raising support for the Nazis.

C2 Explain which sections of society were most important in boosting support for the Nazi Party.

C3 Explain how the appeal of the Nazi Party was attractive to German society as a whole.

How confident do you feel about your answers to these questions? If you are unsure, look again at pages 59–64 for S1–S6; for C1–C3, you could join together with others and discuss a joint answer. Your teacher can provide hints.

2.4 How Hitler became Chancellor, 1932–33

- Examine how Hitler became Chancellor, and understand why it happened.

As 1932 began, the Weimar Republic was crippled by economic problems. The chancellor and leader of the Centre Party, Heinrich Brüning, was struggling to make the constitution of the Republic work. The Reichstag met infrequently and Brüning relied increasingly on presidential decrees to pass laws.

However, Hitler was far from coming to power.

In the general elections of 1930, the Nazi Party had won 107 seats in the Reichstag. This was its largest ever number to that point, but it was only a small portion of the 577 seats available. The Nazis had only received 18% of the votes in the election. Their fierce rivals, the Communist Party, had polled 13% and the moderate Social Democrat Party had polled 25%.

Despite this, within a year, in January 1933, Hitler became Chancellor. How did this happen?

Figure 2.5 gives the outline of events.

Source A

A painting showing a lorry full of Nazi SA stormtroopers driving through a working-class area outside KPD headquarters.

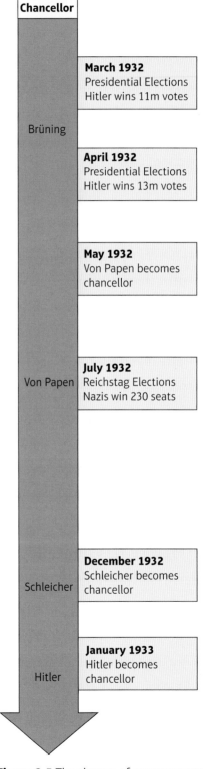

Chancellor

March 1932
Presidential Elections
Hitler wins 11m votes

Brüning

April 1932
Presidential Elections
Hitler wins 13m votes

May 1932
Von Papen becomes
chancellor

July 1932
Von Papen · Reichstag Elections
Nazis win 230 seats

December 1932
Schleicher · Schleicher becomes
chancellor

January 1933
Hitler becomes
Hitler · chancellor

Figure 2.5 The change of governments, 1932–33.

Political developments in 1932

March 1932: Hindenburg stands for re-election

Hindenburg's term of office as President ended in 1932. By this time, he was 84 and increasingly frail, but he was persuaded to stand for election again, to keep the government as stable as possible. Germany was in the depths of depression. Campaigning was bitter and often violent. When the election took place, in March 1932, the results were as follows.

Ernst Thälmann, leader of the KPD	Hindenburg	Adolf Hitler, leader of the NSDAP
5 million votes (14%)	18 million votes (49.6%)	11 million votes (30%)

April 1932: Hindenburg stands for re-election again

No candidate had achieved 50% of the vote, so the election was repeated in April. Hitler campaigned furiously; he rented an aeroplane and flew from town to town delivering speeches. His SA paraded in support of the Nazis and disrupted communist rallies. Political opponents fought in the streets (see Source B). Hindenburg was re-elected, but the results were a serious blow to the communists and a boost to Hitler.

Ernst Thälmann	Hindenburg	Adolf Hitler
4 million votes (11%)	19 million votes (53%)	13 million votes (36%)

30 May 1932: Chancellor Brüning resigns

However, Hindenburg's re-election did not bring stability. In April 1932, the moderate Chancellor, Heinrich Brüning, took two steps which lost him all hope of majority support in the Reichstag.

- First, he banned the SA and SS. There were genuine fears of civil war breaking out on the streets and he wanted to calm unrest and control the Nazis.
- Then he announced a plan to buy up land from the large landowners and use it to house the unemployed.

Source B

A campaign poster in the presidential elections of 1932. It says that Germany would be on the road to self-destruction unless Hindenburg was re-elected.

These two measures united the right-wing groups against Brüning.

- The ban on the SA and SS enraged Hitler. Other political parties feared that their paramilitary groups would also be banned.
- The landowning classes were furious about the plan to buy up their land.
- President Hindenburg, who was a landowning conservative, was furious.

Brüning now had neither the support of the President nor the support of a majority of the Reichstag. Without these he was unable to govern. He resigned on 30 May 1932.

Von Schleicher suggests a new Chancellor

For some time, an ambitious and high-ranking army general, Kurt von Schleicher, had been suggesting a new chancellor to Hindenburg. He had been organising a coalition of right-wing supporters, consisting of landowners, industrialists and army officers. Von Schleicher chose a wealthy gentleman politician, ex-General Franz von Papen (a friend of Hindenburg) as the figurehead for this new coalition.

They did not have a majority in the Reichstag – the moderate Social Democrats were the majority there. Von Schleicher persuaded Hindenburg that if the Nazis, with their huge popular appeal, would support his coalition, it could govern without the Reichstag, using presidential decrees. This was completely against the spirit of the Weimar Republic. The constitution intended that the chancellor should have the support of the majority of the Reichstag. In fact, it was so undemocratic that the new government was known as 'the Cabinet of Barons' (see Interpretation 1).

Interpretation 1

From *The Coming of the Third Reich*, by Richard J. Evans, published in 2004.

These events marked... the end of parliamentary democracy in Germany. Papen and Schleicher saw themselves as creating a 'New State', above parties, indeed opposed to a multi-party system.

Hitler agreed to support the coalition if the ban on the SA was removed. Schleicher's coalition took power.

30 May 1932: von Papen becomes Chancellor

On 30 May 1932, as soon as Brüning resigned, Hindenburg made von Papen Chancellor. Von Schleicher assumed that he could control the Nazis, saying that they were 'merely children who had to be led by the hand'. Nevertheless, Hitler and the Nazi Party were, for the first time, part of the government of Germany.

July 1932: Reichstag elections

Von Papen's new government was in trouble from the start.

In July 1932, there were elections for the Reichstag. Once again, campaigning in June and July caused violence in the streets, mainly between the armed private armies of the Nazi Party and the Communist Party (see Source C). In all, about 100 people were killed and over 7,000 injured. In one clash, near Hamburg, 19 people were killed.

Source C

From *Berlin Stories*, by Christopher Isherwood, published in 1945. Isherwood was a British journalist living in Berlin at the time Hitler came to power in Germany.

*Each week there were new emergency decrees. Brüning's weary episcopal voice issued commands...and was not obeyed... Berlin was in a state of civil war. Hate exploded...out of nowhere; at street corners, in restaurants, cinemas ... at midnight ... in the middle of the afternoon. Knives were whipped out, blows were dealt with spiked rings ... chair-legs, or leaded clubs; bullets slashed the advertisements... In the middle of a crowded street a young man would be attacked... thrashed, and left bleeding on the pavement.'
'[Bruning] is weak" [they] said. "What these swine need is a man with hair on his chest." ... People said that the Nazis would be in power by Christmas.*

When the results were announced, the NSDAP had won 230 seats in the Reichstag. This was a spectacular result.

The Nazi share of the vote had increased from 18% in 1930 to 38% in 1932. The Nazi Party was now the largest party in the Reichstag. Hitler demanded that Hindenburg sack von Papen and appoint him as Chancellor instead.

November 1932: von Papen is sacked

Hindenburg, a field marshal of German forces during the First World War, detested Hitler – in his eyes he was a vulgar, jumped-up corporal. He refused to make Hitler Chancellor. Instead, von Papen hung on to office and called new Reichstag elections in November 1932. He was gambling that Nazi support would fall.

Nazi seats in the Reichstag did fall, to 196, but they were still the largest party. Von Papen's gamble was lost.

At this point, von Schleicher abandoned von Papen. He told Hindenburg that, if von Papen stayed, the country would descend into civil war and the German army would be unable to keep control. Reluctantly, Hindenburg told his friend to resign.

December 1932: von Schleicher becomes Chancellor

Hindenburg was, by now, struggling to find a strong government. But he still refused to make Hitler Chancellor. Von Schleicher told Hindenburg that the November election results showed support for the Nazis was fading. He told a visiting Austrian minister that 'Herr Hitler is no longer a problem; his movement is a thing of the past'. In desperation, on 2 December 1932, Hindenburg appointed von Schleicher as Chancellor.

January 1933: Hitler becomes Chancellor

Von Schleicher's chancellorship had no real political support. With Hitler and the Nazis now against him, von Schleicher was unable to govern. He had no majority in the Reichstag and no support amongst the public. In the face of this, von Schleicher asked Hindenburg to suspend the constitution and make him head of a military dictatorship.

Source D

A 1933 cartoon from the British political magazine *Punch*. It shows Hindenburg (on the left) and von Papen (on the right) lifting Hitler to power.

THE TEMPORARY TRIANGLE.
Von Hindenburg and Von Papen (together)—
"FOR HE'S A JOLLY GOOD FELLOW,
FOR HE'S A JOLLY GOOD FELLOW,
FOR HE'S A JOLLY GOOD FE-EL-LOW,
(Aside: "Confound him!")
AND SO SAY BOTH OF US!"

He said that the German army would support him with armed force. Hindenburg refused.

Rumours began to circulate about Schleicher's plans for an army coup. On 30 January, von Papen told Hindenburg: 'If a new government is not formed by 11 o'clock, the army will march. A military dictatorship under Schleicher looms.'

Von Papen also gave Hindenburg a solution: make Hitler the Chancellor and von Papen the Vice Chancellor. This way, Hindenburg and von Papen thought they could make all the decisions themselves and use Hitler as a figurehead. Von Papen said he had Hitler 'in his pocket' and that 'within two months, we will have pushed Hitler so far into a corner that he'll squeak (like a mouse).' The ageing president finally agreed. As a result, on 30 January 1933, Adolf Hitler was legally appointed the Chancellor of the Weimar Republic.

The roles of Hindenburg, von Schleicher and von Papen

Hitler becoming Chancellor was caused by a range of factors, including Hitler's personal appeal, the policies and organisation of the Nazi Party, the economic collapse of 1929–33 and the long-standing weaknesses of the Weimar Republic. But Hindenburg, von Schleicher and von Papen also had their roles.

- **Hindenburg** never fully supported the idea of a republic. He was a monarchist who preferred the style of government under the Kaiser before 1918. He was therefore quite open to governing by decree, using Article 48, which weakened the Reichstag.

- **Von Schleicher and von Papen** were right-wing conservatives who both wanted to move away from government by the parties elected to the Reichstag and towards a 'stronger' government controlled by wealthy industrialists and landowners. By plotting to replace Brüning with the 'Cabinet of Barons', and advising Hindenburg that he could use the German Army, rather than the Reichstag, to keep his chancellors in power, they undermined the Weimar Republic.

- **All three** underestimated Hitler. They all believed they could bring Hitler and the Nazis into power and then control them. They were wrong.

Activities ?

1 Draw your own timeline, from January 1932 to January 1933. Mark on it all the key events that led to the appointment of Adolf Hitler as Chancellor of Germany.

2 Make a five-column table with the following headings: Brüning, Hitler, Hindenberg, von Schleicher, von Papen. Look through the events of 1932–33, then:

a Jot down details in each column every time one of the key people does anything that eventually leads to Hitler's appointment as Chancellor.

b Write a brief paragraph to summarise who you think was mainly responsible.

3 Hold a class debate about whether it was **people** who brought Hitler to power, or whether it was **factors** such as economic depression and fear of civil war. Then summarise your own view.

THINKING HISTORICALLY Interpretations (4b)

Method is everything: a spectrum of historical methodology

Bad history	Good history
Based on gut feeling	Based on an interpretation of evidence
Argument does not progress logically	Argument progresses logically
No supporting evidence	Evidence used to support argument

Conclusion 1

I think that Hitler becoming Chancellor was a disaster. He had wild policies but people just fell under his spell. So they voted for him. By 1933 he had so many supporters that he forced himself upon the country and became Chancellor. Hindenburg, von Schleicher and von Papen were fools. But they had no alternative. Hitler made them make him Chancellor.

Conclusion 2

Hitler became chancellor in 1933 because of the economic depression. Because they were suffering from unemployment and poverty, people voted for extreme parties like the NSDAP and the KPD. So Hitler became stronger. We can see this from his election results. He did not force himself on the country. But, by 1933, Hindenburg was desperate because von Papen told him there would be a civil war if he did not appoint Hitler as Chancellor.

Conclusion 3

Many factors contributed to Hitler's appointment as Chancellor in 1933. One factor was the economic situation. Unemployment reached six million. This increased poverty and people, in their desperation, voted for extreme parties. By 1932, the NSDAP had 230 seats in the Reichstag. As leader of the biggest party,

Hitler had a good case to be Chancellor. But another factor was the mistakes made by Hindenburg, von Schleicher and von Papen. None of them really wanted a parliamentary democracy. They hoped to create a 'New State' dominated by the wealthy. They thought that, if they included Hitler in their new government, the people of Germany would accept it. They thought they had Hitler 'in their pocket'. They were wrong.

Work in pairs. Read the above conclusions and answer the questions.

1 Look at all the conclusions. In what ways do they differ from one another?

2 Look carefully at the spectrum of historical methodology.

a Where would you place each student's conclusion on the spectrum?

b What evidence would you use to support your choice?

c Suggest one improvement to each conclusion to move it towards 'good' historical writing.

3 How important is it that we know what to look for when we are reading and evaluating historical writing?

Exam-style question, Section B

Study Source B (page 68) and Source C (page 69).

How useful are Sources B and C for an enquiry into the strength of democracy in Germany by 1932?

Explain your answer, using Sources B and C and your knowledge of the historical context. **8 marks**

Exam tip

A good answer will consider:

- how useful the information in each source for this particular enquiry is
- how the provenance (i.e. the type of source, its origin, author or purpose) of each source affects how useful it is
- how knowledge of the historical context affects a judgement of how useful each source is.

Summary

- By the start of 1932, Hitler still had little political power.
- However, in January 1933, he was appointed Chancellor of the Weimar Republic.
- One reason was Hitler's success in the presidential elections of 1932.
- Another reason was the success of the NSDAP in the Reichstag elections of 1932.
- A further reason was that conservative politicians such as von Schleicher and von Papen plotted to remove Chancellor Brüning and reduce the power of the Reichstag.
- Von Schleicher and von Papen both thought that they could include Hitler and the Nazis in their governments and then control them.
- There was a general fear that civil war might break out if Germany could not find a strong government with widespread popular support.
- President Hindenburg resisted the idea of Hitler as Chancellor, but eventually agreed.

Checkpoint

Strengthen

S1 Describe the events of the presidential elections of March and April 1932.

S2 Describe how Brüning lost his position as German Chancellor.

S3 Describe how von Papen came to power as German Chancellor.

S4 Describe the results of the Reichstag elections of July 1932.

S5 Describe how von Papen was replaced by von Schleicher in December 1932.

S6 Describe how von Schleicher was replaced by Hitler in January 1933.

Challenge

C1 Identify the factors that helped Hitler become Chancellor in 1933.

C2 Weigh up which of these factors was the most important.

C3 Explain the roles of Hindenburg, von Schleicher and von Papen in Hitler gaining the chancellorship in 1933.

How confident do you feel about your answers to these questions? If you are unsure, look again at pages 67–70 for S1–S6; for C1–C3, you could join together with others and discuss a joint answer. Your teacher can provide hints.

Recap: Hitler's rise to power, 1919–33

Recall quiz

1 What was the full (English) name of the DAP?

2 What was the full (English) name of the NSDAP?

3 What was *Der Stürmer*?

4 What was Hitler's *Stosstrupp*?

5 What is the meaning of the word *Putsch* in Munich Putsch?

6 Who was elected as the German president in 1925?

7 Who was the German Chancellor from 1930 to 1932?

8 Who was the German Chancellor from May to November 1932?

9 Who became the German Chancellor in December 1932?

10 Who became the German Chancellor in January 1933?

Activities

1 In February 1920, Hitler and the DAP produced the Twenty-Five Point Programme. Page 43 lists nine of these. List as many as you can.

2 Hitler attracted supporters to the DAP because of his appeal as a speaker. Page 44 lists three things that made him effective as a speaker. Name them.

3 Hitler improved the organisation of the DAP. Complete the following sentences that explain some of the ways he did this.

　a Rudolf Schüssler was…

　b The new name for the DAP was…

　c The swastika and the straight arm salute were…

　d The *Völkischer Beobachter* was…

4 In one sentence, explain how each of these people contributed to the early stages of the Nazi Party.

　a Rudolf Hess

　b Hermann Goering

　c Julius Streicher

　d Ernst Röhm

5 Make a list of six things that you know about the SA (Sturmabteilung).

6 In one sentence each, give one long-term, one medium-term and one short-term cause of the Munich Putsch of 1923.

7 Make a timeline of the events of the Munich Putsch from the evening of 8 November to the end of 9 November 1923.

8 List three reasons why the Munich Putsch could be considered a failure and three reasons why it could be considered a success.

9 Briefly describe these features of Hitler's beliefs, as described in *Mein Kampf*:

　a nationalism

　b socialism

　c totalitarianism

　d traditional German values

10 Briefly describe these features of the Nazi Party after 1924:

　a party headquarters and national organisation

　b SS (*Schutzstaffel*)

　c Bamberg Conference, 1926

11 'The Nazi Party had achieved very limited success by the end of 1928'. Give three facts that support this statement.

12 Briefly explain to a friend what the Great Depression of 1929 was and how it affected Germany.

13 Support for the Nazi Party increased, 1929–33. Explain their appeal to the following groups:

　a the owners of big businesses

　b the working class

　c the middle class

　d farmers

　e young people

　f women

14 Explain how the Nazi Party appealed to **all** Germans, not just individual groups or classes.

15 Sketch a timeline of events from January 1932 to January 1933 to show how Hitler became Chancellor of the Weimar Republic.

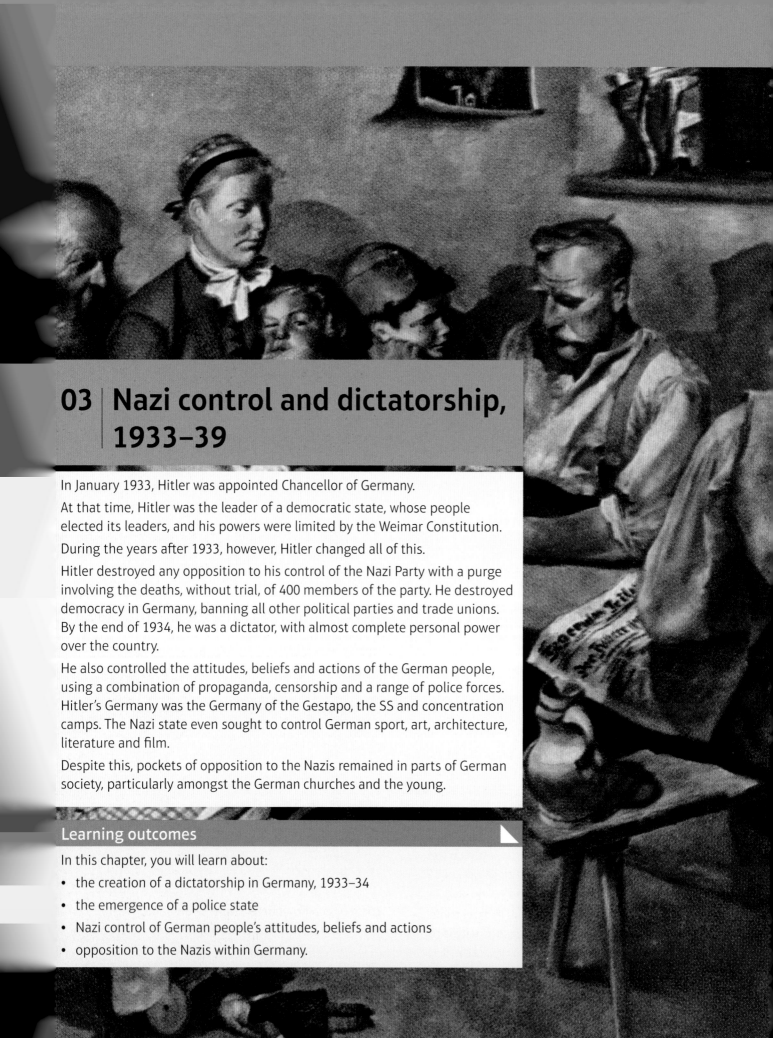

03 | Nazi control and dictatorship, 1933–39

In January 1933, Hitler was appointed Chancellor of Germany.

At that time, Hitler was the leader of a democratic state, whose people elected its leaders, and his powers were limited by the Weimar Constitution.

During the years after 1933, however, Hitler changed all of this.

Hitler destroyed any opposition to his control of the Nazi Party with a purge involving the deaths, without trial, of 400 members of the party. He destroyed democracy in Germany, banning all other political parties and trade unions. By the end of 1934, he was a dictator, with almost complete personal power over the country.

He also controlled the attitudes, beliefs and actions of the German people, using a combination of propaganda, censorship and a range of police forces. Hitler's Germany was the Germany of the Gestapo, the SS and concentration camps. The Nazi state even sought to control German sport, art, architecture, literature and film.

Despite this, pockets of opposition to the Nazis remained in parts of German society, particularly amongst the German churches and the young.

Learning outcomes

In this chapter, you will learn about:

- the creation of a dictatorship in Germany, 1933–34
- the emergence of a police state
- Nazi control of German people's attitudes, beliefs and actions
- opposition to the Nazis within Germany.

3.1 The creation of a dictatorship, 1933–34

Learning outcomes

- Understand the events surrounding the Reichstag fire, and the significance of it.
- Understand how Hitler gained more power with the introduction of the Enabling Act, and his removal of opposition groups.
- Understand the events surrounding the Night of the Long Knives.

From 30 January 1933, Hitler was Chancellor of Germany. But his power was limited.

- The Weimar constitution controlled what the Chancellor could do.
- Hindenburg retained all the powers of the President.
- Hitler's cabinet had 12 members – but only two were NSDAP members (Wilhelm Frick and Hermann Goering).
- NSDAP members numbered only about one-third of the Reichstag.

Most people thought other politicians would restrain Hitler. The *New York Times* observed that 'the composition of the Cabinet leaves Herr Hitler no scope for his dictatorial ambition'. But they were wrong. Hitler was looking for a chance to increase his own power. His first opportunity to do so was created by a fire at the Reichstag.

The Reichstag Fire

On the evening of 27 February 1933, the Reichstag building was destroyed by a massive fire. A young Dutchman, a communist supporter named Marinus van der Lubbe, was caught on the site with matches and firelighters. He confessed and was put on trial with four others, though he claimed that he had acted alone. The other four were found not guilty and released; van der Lubbe was found guilty and executed. But the fire also had wider significance.

Van der Lubbe's execution was not enough for Hitler. He and Hermann Goering, the new chief of police, claimed that van der Lubbe was part of a communist conspiracy against the government. They decided to use the Reichstag Fire as an opportunity to attack the communists.

Source A

From the memoirs of Rudolf Diels, Head of the Prussian Police, published in 1950. Diels was in charge of questioning van der Lubbe. Here he is recalling Hitler's reaction to the Reichstag Fire in 1933.

Hitler... started screaming at the top of his voice. "Now we'll show them! The German people have been soft too long. Every Communist official must be shot. All Communist deputies must be hanged tonight. All friends of the Communists must be locked up. And that goes for the Social Democrats too.

Source B

A cartoon from the German magazine *Kladderdatsch* in 1933. *Kladdertatsch* was a satirical magazine which put forward strong opinions on political events. This illustration shows Joseph Goebbels, pulling evidence of a communist plot out of a box.

Source C

A photograph taken inside the Reichstag soon after the Reichstag Fire.

Four thousand communists were arrested on the night of the Reichstag Fire. The next day, Hitler used the fire to pressurise Hindenburg into declaring a state of emergency. As long as Hindenburg supported him, Hitler could now use decrees to govern Germany. Next, he persuaded Hindenburg to call an election for 5 March 1933. He hoped for more Nazi seats in the Reichstag. There was nothing unconstitutional about any of this.

However, before the election of March 1933 took place, Hitler did various things.

- Hitler issued the Decree for the Protection of the People and the State. This gave him powers to imprison political opponents and ban communist newspapers.
- Since he now controlled Germany's police force, Hitler could ensure that they turned a blind eye to the violent activities of the SA.

- Hitler persuaded Gustav Krupp and other industrialists to bankroll the Nazi campaign. Three million marks were donated in just one meeting.

It was a bloody election campaign; violent clashes led to 70 deaths.

When the results were announced, the Nazis increased their Reichstag members to 288. Hitler used his emergency powers to ban the Communist Party from taking up its 81 seats. With the support of the other nationalist parties, this gave Hitler a two-thirds majority in the Reichstag.

This was crucial. Hitler now had enough votes to change the constitution of the Republic.

THINKING HISTORICALLY — Thinking Historically – Evidence (3b)

It depends on the question

When considering the usefulness of historical sources, people often consider 'reliability' (whether a witness can be trusted). This is important. However, some sources are not witnesses – they are simply the remains of the past.

Work in small groups.

1 Imagine you are investigating the impact of the Reichstag Fire on politics in Germany.

   a Write at least two statements that you can reasonably infer about the impact of the Reichstag Fire on politics in Germany based solely on Source C.

   b Which of your statements are you most sure of? Explain your answer.

2 Source B is unreliable testimony – it is a political cartoon which was deliberately giving a provocative view of events. However, try to think of at least two statements that you can still reasonably infer about the impact of the Reichstag Fire on politics in Germany, using this source.

3 Which source is more useful for investigating the impact of the Reichstag Fire on politics in Germany? Explain your answer.

4 In your group, discuss the following question and write down your thoughts. How are reliability and usefulness related?

The Enabling Act

In March 1933, Hitler proposed the Enabling Act to the Reichstag. Since this Act was designed to destroy the power of the Reichstag, Hitler expected opposition and used his Nazi Party stormtroopers to intimidate his opponents.

The full name of the law proposed by Hitler was the *Law for the Removal of the Distress of the People and Reich*. It said that:

- the Reich Cabinet could pass new laws
- these laws could overrule the constitution of the Weimar Republic
- the laws would be proposed by the Chancellor – Hitler.

In effect, the Enabling Act would change the constitution. It would give Hitler the right to make laws for four years without the consent of the Reichstag. The Reichstag vote was taken under very threatening circumstances (see Source E).

Source D

From an official report by the SPD about the raid on their Braunschweig branch in March 1933.

The Nazis broke windows and came through the holes. They opened fire; the office marketing manager was shot in the stomach. Secretaries were driven with clubs and daggers and locked up for hours. The regular police blocked off the surrounding streets. The Nazis looted the building under their very eyes.

Source E

From *Knaves, Fools and Heroes* by Sir John Wheeler-Bennet, published in 1974. Wheeler-Bennet lived in Germany in 1934. Here, he is recalling the debate on the Enabling Act.

There were nearly 300 Nazi deputies and 50 or so Nationalist. There was a marked absence of Communists. There were fewer Social Democrats than could have been present, because some were in hospital, the victims of electoral violence; some had fled the country — and who could blame them?

Along the corridors, SS men, in their sinister black and silver uniforms, had been posted; their legs apart and arms crossed, their eyes fixed and cruel, looking like messengers of doom.

Outside, a mob of SA chanted threatening slogans: 'Give us the Bill or else fire and murder'. Their clamour was clearly audible within the chamber.

On 24 March 1933, in the absence of any communist members, the Reichstag passed the Enabling Act by 444 votes to 94. It was supported by the Nazis, the National Party and the Centre Party. In this sense, it was legal – even though Reichstag members were intimidated during the vote.

The Act was renewed in 1937. In effect, therefore, the 1933 Enabling Act marked the end of democratic rule and the end of the Weimar constitution.

Removing other opposition

Once Hitler had the power to pass laws without consulting the Reichstag, he set about removing other sources of opposition.

Trade unions

Trade unions were potential sources of opposition to Hitler. Hitler believed that, if communists amongst working men were able to control their trade unions, then these could be used to undermine the government (for example, in strikes). Therefore, in May 1933:

- Nazis broke into trade union offices all over Germany and arrested trade union officials
- Hitler used his new powers to ban trade unions and made strikes illegal.

Political parties

Hitler then began to remove all political opposition.

- In May 1933, he attacked his two main political rivals. Nazi stormtroopers entered the offices of the Social Democratic Party and the Communist Party, destroyed their newspapers and confiscated all their funds.
- Two months later, in July 1933, Hitler followed this up by issuing a decree to make all political parties in Germany illegal, except for the NSDAP (see Source F).

Source F

Law against the Establishment of Parties, 14 July 1933.

Article I The National Socialist German Workers' Party constitutes the only political party in Germany.

Article II Whoever undertakes to maintain the organisation of another political party or to form a new political party shall be punished with penal servitude of up to three years or imprisonment of between six months and three years.

Source G

A British cartoon from July 1933, published in the *Daily Express*. It is showing President Hindenburg in the middle of a boxing ring holding up Hitler's hand in triumph. The defeated opponent in the corner is 'German Liberties'.

Local government

The next step was for Hitler to strengthen the central government in Berlin – which he controlled – and to weaken local government in Germany.

Under the Weimar constitution, each region (Land) of Germany had its own parliament, which ran the local government in the area. By 1934, Hitler had control of the Reichstag – but he could not control the 18 Länder parliaments.

So, in January 1934, he abolished the Länder parliaments and declared instead that governors, appointed by him, would run every region of Germany.

Activities ?

1 Here is a list of events which strengthened Hitler's control of Germany. Create a timeline for 1933 and 1934 (you will complete it on page 81) and mark the following events:

  a Hitler becomes Chancellor

  b The Reichstag Fire – state of national emergency declared by Hindenburg

  c An election for new members of the Reichstag

  d The Enabling Act passed

  e Trade Unions banned

  f All political parties banned, except NSDAP

  g Länder parliaments abolished.

2 Which of these events were legal and which were illegal? Discuss with a partner and mark your decisions on your timeline.

3 Discuss with a partner what you think is the meaning of the metal swastika shown in Source G, which Goering is removing from Hitler's boxing glove.

4 Between January 1933 and January 1934, was Hitler's growing power gained by legal or illegal means? Write a paragraph to explain your view. Leave a space at the end to add to your answer later.

The Night of the Long Knives

By the start of 1934, Hitler had made Germany a one-party state – the Nazi Party. He now made sure that he was the unrivalled leader of the party.

Ernst Röhm, the leader of the SA, was a threat to Hitler – or, at least, Hitler believed that he was.

- Röhm had merged an army veterans group, the Stahlhelm, with the SA. This brought SA numbers to three million. Some stormtroopers complained that although they risked death for Hitler, he undervalued them. In addition, by 1933, 60% of the SA were permanently unemployed. These embittered SA members were loyal to Röhm, which put him in an ideal position to challenge Hitler.

- Röhm also opposed Hitler's policies. He criticised Hitler's links with rich industrialists and army generals (see Source H). He wanted more socialist policies, to tax the rich and help the working class.

Source H

From the book *Hitler Speaks*, published in 1940, by Hermann Rauschning, a Nazi official who emigrated from Germany in 1936. Here, he is quoting words spoken by Ernst Röhm, when he was drunk in 1934.

Adolf is a swine. His old friends are not good enough for him. Adolf is turning into a gentleman. He wants to sit on a hilltop and pretend he is God.

Others thought that Röhm was a threat too.

- German army officers were worried about Röhm. After the Versailles Treaty, the army had only 100,000 men, whereas the SA was much bigger. They believed that Röhm wanted the SA to replace the German army.

- Leaders of the SS, such as Heinrich Himmler and Reinhard Heydrich, resented Röhm too. They wanted to reduce the power of the SA, so that they could increase their own power and the status of the SS.

In 1934, leaders of the SS and the army warned Hitler that Röhm was planning to seize power.

As a result of all this, Hitler arranged to remove the threat of Röhm and the SA. He arranged a meeting with Röhm and 100 other SA leaders at a hotel in the Bavarian town of Bad Wiessee on 30 June 1934. When they arrived, Röhm and the other senior officers of the SA were arrested, imprisoned and shot (see Source I). This event is known as **the Night of the Long Knives**.

Source I

Extracts from the diary of Alfred Rosenberg from 30 June 1934. Rosenberg was a leading Nazi.

With an SS escort, the Führer knocked gently on Roehm's door: 'A message from Munich', he said in a disguised voice. 'Come in' Roehm shouted, 'the door is open'. Hitler tore open the door, fell on Roehm as he lay in bed, seized him by the throat and screamed, 'You are under arrest, you pig!' Then he turned him over to the SS.

Interpretation 1

From *Life in Germany 1919–1945*, by Steve Waugh, published in 2009.

The greatest threat came from within the Nazi Party… Röhm, as leader of the SA, was a genuine threat to Hitler's own position as leader. Röhm was the commander of a very large organisation of men whose members were increasingly violent and out of control… Moreover, Röhm favoured a 'second revolution'… which would lead to more socialist policies. The purge was also the result of a power struggle (between Röhm and) leading Nazis, like Herman Goering, the leader of the SS.

Interpretation 2

From *Germany 1918–45*, by G. Lacey and K. Shephard, published in 1971.

The smoothness with which the murders of 30 June were carried out is powerful proof that no Röhm plot was imminent. There was no resistance encountered anywhere. Many victims unsuspectingly surrendered voluntarily, believing it was a big mistake. The only shots fired were those of the executioners.

Extend your knowledge

More murders

Röhm was taken to Stadelheim Prison, where, on 1 July, an SS Brigade Leader arrived. He left a pistol loaded with one bullet in Röhm's cell, inviting suicide. After 15 minutes, hearing no sound, he entered the cell with his deputy and they both shot him.

In addition to Röhm, at Stadelheim six other SA leaders were shot on Hitler's orders.

Over a four-day period, about 400 people, including 150 senior members of the SA, were shot without trial. Leading politicians were also murdered. These included General von Schleicher – the ex-Chancellor – who was gunned down, along with his wife. Goering announced they had been shot resisting arrest. Gregor Strasser, a Nazi with socialist views similar to Röhm, was locked in a Gestapo cell before gunmen sprayed bullets through a window. A lone gunman entered to finish him off.

Why do you think that murders like these benefitted Hitler?

The killing continues

During the Night of the Long Knives, von Papen (still Vice Chancellor), protested to Goering. Von Papen was told that the SS had things under control and he should return home for his own safety. SS squads were rounding up suspects; one group reached von Papen's office before he did, shot his press secretary and arrested his staff. Von Papen's home was surrounded and his telephone cut off. It was now clear that he did not have 'Hitler in his pocket'.

Hitler was now acting illegally, murdering his rivals for power. At a press conference on 2 July 1934, Goering announced that the security forces had been monitoring Röhm for months. They had discovered that he was planning a 'second revolution' to replace Hitler, and so, he said, the killings were in the best interests of Germany.

Source J

A speech by Hitler in the Reichstag, on 13 July 1934.

```
I ordered the leaders of the guilty to be shot. If anyone
asks why I did not use the courts of justice, I say this:
in this hour, I was responsible for the fate of the German
people and I became the supreme judge of the German people.
```

Some Germans objected to the violence, but few knew how bad it was. Most were grateful that the SA, hated for their brutality, had been restrained. The SA continued after 1934, but it was limited to giving muscle to the Nazi party and no longer rivalled the army. It was also now firmly under Hitler's control.

Source K

Heinrich Himmler, head of the SS, at the front on the right, with Ernst Röhm, leader of the SA in 1933.

Exam-style question, Section B

Study Interpretations 1 and 2 (page 80).

They give different views about the threat which Röhm posed to Hitler in 1934. What is the main difference between these views?

Explain your answer, using details from both interpretations.

4 marks

Exam tip

It is not enough just to find differences of detail between the interpretations.

The key is:

- to decide how the view in one interpretation is different from the other
- use the detail in each interpretation to illustrate how the views differ.

The Death of Hindenburg

On 2 August 1934, President Hindenburg died, aged 87. Hitler took over supreme power.

- He declared himself Germany's Führer and decreed that, as Führer, he would add all of the President's powers to those he already held as Chancellor.
- He forced an oath of loyalty to him from every soldier in the army.

A plebiscite (public vote) was held on 19 August to confirm Hitler as the Führer. Bombarded by pro-Nazi propaganda, 90% of voters voted in favour. The Weimar Republic had formally ended. Hitler's Third Reich had begun.

Activities

1 Complete the timeline which you started on page 79 by adding the following events:
   a The Night of the Long Knives
   b The death of Hindenburg
   c Hitler becomes Führer
2 Discuss with a partner whether these were legal or illegal and mark this on your timeline.
3 By August 1934, was Hitler's political power based on legal or illegal means? Add to the answer which you started on page 79, to give your overall conclusion. Make sure that you explain and justify your answer.

Summary

- The Reichstag Fire gave Hitler the opportunity to begin creating a dictatorship in Germany.
- After the fire, there were open attacks on communists and the Nazis gained more seats in the Reichstag.
- The Enabling Act changed Germany's constitution. It gave much more power to Hitler. As Chancellor, he and his Cabinet could pass laws without the support of the Reichstag. The Night of the Long Knives, which saw many senior officers in the SA killed, enabled Hitler to strengthen his control of the Nazi Party.
- After the death of Hindenburg, Hitler moved to take power. On 19 August, the Weimar Republic formally ended.

Checkpoint

Strengthen

S1 Describe the events of the Reichstag Fire.

S2 What events led up to the passing of the Enabling Act?

S3 Describe the details of the Enabling Act and laws limiting unions and political parties.

S4 What was the Night of the Long Knives?

Challenge

C1 In what ways was Hitler politically stronger by the end of 1934 than in early 1933?

How confident do you feel about your answers to these questions? If you are unsure, look again at pages 75–80 for S1 to S4; for C1, discuss with others and consider a joint answer. Your teacher can provide hints.

3.2 The police state

Learning outcomes

- Understand the different aspects of the Nazi police state, including controlling Germany's legal and religious systems.
- Examine how far Hitler succeeded in creating a police state.

The German state which Hitler created after 1933 was a **police state**. This was a state in which the Nazi government used the police – often the secret police – to control what people did and what they said. People who did or said anything to harm the state or the Nazi Party were punished. The police state was a means of keeping control.

When Hitler became Chancellor in January 1933, Germany already had a police force. It was controlled by central government, but run by local authorities in Germany's states and towns. In January 1933, Hitler's control of government was still weak, so he realised that his control of the police was also weak.

Hitler therefore set up his own police and security forces. These were not run by the government. They were run by the Nazi Party and accountable to Hitler. Their role was to protect and support the Nazi Party.

Policing the police state

The main organisations used by Hitler to control this Nazi police state were the SS, the SD and the Gestapo. At first, these were separate Nazi organisations. Gradually, however, they were organised into a structure.

**SS
(Protection Squad)
Heinrich Himmler**
Black uniforms. By 1936, the SS controlled all Germany's police and security forces.

**SD
(Security Service)
Reinhard Heydrich**
Uniformed. Spied on all known opponents and critics of the Nazi Party and the German government.

**Gestapo
(Secret State Police)
Reinhard Heydrich**
No uniforms.
Prosecuted anyone who said or did anything critical of the Nazis or the government.
Relied mainly on informants. Feared by the general public.

Figure 3.1 The structure of the Nazi police state.

The SS

The SS (*Schutzstaffel* or Protection Squad) was originally a military group of 240 men, set up in 1925 as a personal bodyguard for Hitler. From 1929, it was run by Heinrich Himmler. In 1932, it was given its famous black uniforms, to distinguish it from the 'Brownshirts' – the stormtroopers of the SA.

In the early 1930s the main role of the SS was as the Nazi Party's own private police force. They were totally loyal to Hitler and Himmler. It was the SS who warned Hitler about Röhm in 1934 and Hitler used SS officers to murder SA leaders during the Night of the Long Knives.

During the 1930s, the SS was expanded to 240,000 men and put in charge of all the other police and security services. Himmler did not believe that the SS were obliged to act within the law (see Source A).

Source A

Himmler addressing the Committee for Police Law in 1936.

It does not matter in the least if our actions are against some clause in the law; in my work for the Führer and the nation, I do what my conscience and common sense tells me is right.

Himmler was very particular about recruitment to the SS. He wanted examples of perfect German manhood; they were expected to marry 'racially pure' wives to create 'racially pure' Germans for the future (see Source B).

Source B

Himmler, speaking to SS commanders, 18 February 1937.

In the SS we have about one case of homosexuality a month. They will be publicly degraded, expelled, and handed over to the courts... they will be sent to a concentration camp, and shot, while attempting to escape. Thereby, the healthy blood which we are cultivating for Germany, will be kept pure.

The SD

The SD (*Sicherheitsdienst* or Security Force) was originally formed in 1931 by Heinrich Himmler, head of the SS, as a security force for the Nazi Party to monitor its opponents. He made Reinhard Heydrich its leader.

The SD kept a card index with details of everyone it suspected of opposing the Nazi Party or the German government at home or abroad. These were not kept at any government building, but at Brown House, the headquarters of the Nazi Party in Munich.

The Gestapo (*Geheime Staatspolizei* or State Secret Police)

The Gestapo was Hitler's non-uniformed secret police force. They were set up in 1933 by Hermann Goering. However, in 1934, it was placed under SS control and, in 1936, Heydrich became its leader. So, from 1936, Hitler had created a unified police and security force, with the SS and the SD and the Gestapo working in parallel to it.

The main aim of the Gestapo was to identify anyone who criticised or opposed the Nazi government (see Sources C and D). They spied on people, tapped their phones and used networks of informants to identify suspects. In 1939 alone, 160,000 people were arrested for political offences. The Gestapo were officially given permission to use torture when questioning suspects or gaining confessions.

Source C

Instructions to the Gestapo from their deputy chief, Werner Best.

Any attempt to... uphold different ideas will be ruthlessly dealt with, as the symptoms of an illness which threatens the healthy unity of the state. To discover the enemies of the state, watch them and render them harmless is the duty of the political police.

The main weapon of the Gestapo was fear. Germans particularly feared the Gestapo, because they could not tell them apart from other members of the public. The Gestapo often arrived early in the morning to take suspects away, offenders could be imprisoned without trial and many families received letters saying that their relatives had died in custody. Many were sent to concentration camps, which were large prisons with often inhumane conditions. When rumours leaked out about conditions in the concentration camps, fear of the Gestapo grew even more.

Arguably, fear of Hitler's police forces was even more powerful than the police forces themselves. There were never more than 30,000 Gestapo to police a population of about 80 million; in some large towns, such as Hamburg, there were fewer than 50 officers, and most of these were clerical staff.

Source D

A photograph of Nazi stormtroopers in the German city of Stuttgart. Their banner reads 'We won't tolerate sabotage of the work of the Führer'.

Interpretation 1

From *The Nazis: A Warning from History*, by Laurence Rees, published in 2005.

Like all modern policing systems, the Gestapo was only as good or bad as the co-operation it received – and the files reveal that it received a high level of co-operation. Only around 10% of political crimes committed… were actually discovered by the Gestapo; another 10% were passed on to the Gestapo by the regular police or the Nazi Party. Around 80% was discovered by ordinary citizens who turned the information over… Most of this unpaid cooperation came from people who were not members of the Nazi Party – they were 'ordinary' citizens.

Exam-style question, Section A

Explain why the Nazi police state was successful between 1933-39

You may use the following in your answer:

• the Gestapo

• concentration camps.

You must also use information of your own. **12 marks**

Exam tip

Focus on explaining 'why'. Aim to give at least three clear reasons.

Concentration camps

By 1939, 150,000 people were 'under protective arrest' in prisons. This means that they had not committed criminal acts such as stealing. Instead, they were locked up for doing things that the Nazis disapproved of, such as voicing views opposed to Hitler and the Nazis.

To cope with the growing number of people who were arrested, new prisons were created, which were run by the SA and the SS. These were called **concentration camps**.

- The first Nazi concentration camp was opened at Dachau in 1933.
- Later that year, the first camp for women was opened at Moringen.
- Camps were located in isolated areas, away from cities and the publics gaze.

The inmates of the concentration camps were:

- 'undersirables', such as prostitutes or homosexuals,
- minority groups, such as Jews, of whom the Nazis disapproved
- political prisoners – people whom the Nazis feared would undermine their control of Germany, including intellectuals, communists or political writers (see Source E).

Source E

A photograph of Carl von Ossietzky, a journalist and critic of the Nazis, at Esterwegen concentration camp in 1935.

Controlling the legal system

Another way that Hitler controlled his police state was by controlling what happened within the legal system. Hitler realised that his opponents stood little chance of success if trumped-up charges could be brought against them and then they were tried in courts which were biased in favour of the Nazis.

Controlling the judges

Firstly, Hitler set up the National Socialist League for the Maintenance of the Law. He insisted that all judges must be members. If any judges displeased the Nazis, they were denied membership. This way, Hitler could ensure that all judges would support Nazi ideas. Judges were instructed that, in any conflict between the interests of the Nazi Party and the law, the interests of the Nazi Party were more important (see Source F).

Source F

A speech by Hans Frank from 1936. Hitler appointed Frank as President of the German Academy of Law.

The basis for interpreting all legal sources is the Nazi philosophy, especially as expressed in the party programme and in the speeches of our Führer.

Controlling the law courts

Next, Hitler abolished trial by jury. Judges decided innocence, guilt and punishments.

Finally, Hitler set up a new People's Court, to hear all cases of treason– offences against the state. Judges for this court were hand-picked and trials were held in secret. Hitler sometimes imposed sentences himself (see Source G). There was no right to appeal against the verdict of the People's Court. Between 1934 and 1939, 534 people were sentenced to death for political offences. Between 1930 and 1932, only eight people had been sentenced in this manner.

Source G

A letter from Hitler's private office, sent to the Gestapo. Luftgas was 74 years old. He had been convicted of hoarding eggs soon after the start of the Second World War.

The Führer has seen the press cutting about the sentencing of the Jew, Markus Luftgas, to 2½ years in prison. He desires that Luftgas should be executed. Please make the arrangements.

Extend your knowledge

Roland Freisler

Roland Freisler was a judge in the People's Court. He became well known for bullying defendants, shouting over their attempts to speak and verbally abusing them. About 90% of the defendants whose cases were heard by Freisler received the death penalty.

Activities

1 Write a list of three ways in which Hitler used the legal system to control Nazi Germany.

2 Historians sometimes say that, in the 1930s, the law in Germany was 'Nazified'. Hold a class discussion to decide what this might mean, then write a paragraph to explain your answer.

Controlling religious views

The Christian religion was another aspect of German society which Hitler's Nazi police state set out to control. The likelihood of friction was obvious. Whereas the Nazis glorified strength and violence and taught racial superiority, Christianity preached tolerance and peace and respect for all people. At first, Hitler tried to control the Christian churches by reassuring them and encouraging them to work with the Nazi government (see Sources H and I). However, this did not work for long. Soon, he turned the full force of the police state against Christians.

Source H

Extracts from a speech by Hitler in the Reichstag on the Enabling Law, March 1933.

Christianity is the unshakeable foundation of the moral and ethical life of our people. The National Government's concern will be for cooperation of the Church with the State. It expects, however that (this) will meet with similar appreciation from their side.

The Catholic Church

One-third of Germany's Christians were Catholic. There were obvious sources of friction between Catholicism and Nazism.

- On social issues, Catholics owed their first allegiance to the Pope, rather than Hitler.
- Catholics also had their own schools, which taught values different from Nazi state schools.

Trying, at first, to reach agreement with the Catholic Church, in July 1933, Hitler reached a **concordat** (agreement) with the Pope.

- Hitler agreed to confirm freedom of worship for Catholics and not to interfere with Catholic schools in Germany.
- The Catholic Church agreed that its priests would not interfere in politics and ordered German bishops to swear loyalty to the National Socialist regime (see Source J).

However, Hitler did not keep his promise to the Catholic Church. As the 1930s went on:

Source I

An NSDAP poster from 1933 showing the swastika knocking out the Catholics and the Communists.

Source J

Extract from the oath of allegiance to the Nazi regime, sworn by German Catholic bishops in 1933.

In my spiritual office, for the welfare and interest of the German Reich, I will endeavour to avoid all detrimental acts which might endanger it.

- Catholic priests were harassed and arrested – many ended up in concentration camps
- Catholic schools were brought in line with state schools or closed
- Catholic youth activities, such as the Catholic Youth League, were banned.

By 1937, Pope Pius XI realised that the concordat was worthless. He issued a stinging criticism of the Nazi regime in a statement known as 'Mit Brennender Sorge' ('With Burning Anxiety').

Source K

A French cartoon from 1933. The Pope is shown on the right, encouraging a priest to accept Hitler.

The Protestant Church

At first, some Protestants were so grateful that Hitler had protected them from anti-Christian Communists that they worked with the Nazis (see Source L).

The Reich Church, 1936

The Protestant churches which favoured working with the Nazis combined in 1936 to form a single Protestant church called the Reich Church. Its leader was Ludwig Müller. Hitler made Müller the Reich Bishop of Germany.

- Protestant pastors who supported Hitler's views were allowed to continue providing church services.
- Some Protestant pastors even allowed the Nazi swastika to be displayed in their churches.
- The Nazis insisted that Jews should not be baptised into the Reich Church and that the Jewish teachings of the Old Testament should be excluded from Christian teaching.

However, not all Protestants accepted the Nazi state. A few even spoke out against Hitler. The most famous of these was Pastor Martin Niemöller. In 1933, he was one of the Protestant pastors who set up the Pastors' Emergency League (PEL) to campaign against Nazi actions. But, in 1937, Niemöller was sent to a concentration camp and the PEL was banned (see pages 100–101 for details).

Source L

A statement from a German Protestant church leader in June 1937.

We all know that, if the Third Reich were to collapse, Communism would come in its place. So, we must show loyalty to the Führer, who has saved us from Communism and given us a better chance.

How far did Hitler succeed?

Hitler tried, at first, to work with the Christian churches. However, he ended up in conflict with them and tried to make them conform to Nazi ideas. Just like the police and the law courts, they became 'Nazified'. In all areas in which Hitler tried to control Germans, there were some who opposed him (see page 99, for example).

As a result of all this, Germany was gradually becoming a **totalitarian state** – a country where the government controlled all sections of the state, including the Reichstag, the NSDAP, the army, the police and the legal system.

Activities

1   Work with a partner to identify and write down:

  a   three examples of Nazi Germany co-operating with the Christian churches

  b   five examples of the Christian churches being oppressed in Nazi Germany.

2   Pages 83–89 are all about ways in which Hitler controlled Germany, using police, prisons, courts and religious restrictions. Create a diagram, containing all these key areas showing how they combined to create Hitler's police state.

Summary

- Nazi Germany was a police state, controlled by the SS, SD and Gestapo.
- From 1933, concentration camps were also used to deal with 'undesirables', such as political opponents of Nazism.
- The legal system was 'Nazified' – it was made to work in the interests of the Nazi Party. Law courts and judges were placed under the direct control of the Nazis.
- Religion was also closely controlled, although there was some resistance to this, from both Catholics and Protestants.

Checkpoint

Strengthen

S1 Describe the key features of the SS, SD, Gestapo and concentration camps.

S2 How did the Nazi Party control Germany's legal system?

S3 How did the Nazi Party try to control religion in Germany?

Challenge

C1 Explain, with detailed examples, why Nazi Germany is called a police state.

C2 Explain, with detailed examples, why Nazi Germany is called a totalitarian state.

How confident do you feel about your answers to these questions? If you are unsure, look again at pages 83–86 for S1, page 87 for S2 and pages 88–89 for S3; for C1 and C2, join together with others and discuss a joint answer. Your teacher can provide hints.

3.3 Controlling and influencing attitudes

Learning outcomes

- Understand how Goebbels used propaganda to control and influence German people.
- Understand how the Nazis used media, sport, rallies, culture and the Arts to control and influence German people.

In Hitler's totalitarian state, the Nazi Party sought to control and influence the attitudes of the German public. It did this by:

- censorship*
- propaganda*
- controlling culture and the Arts.

Key terms

Censorship*

Censorship involves banning information or ideas. It sometimes involves banning the vehicles for delivering ideas, such as newspapers, pictures, radio or film. Censorship therefore controls attitudes by *forbidding* certain information or opinions.

Propaganda*

Propaganda is another way of controlling attitudes, but propaganda doesn't ban opinions, it *creates* them. Propaganda uses vehicles for information and ideas, such as newspapers, posters, radio and film, to put ideas into people's minds and therefore shape attitudes.

Goebbels and propaganda

Joseph Goebbels was the key person in the Nazi efforts to control and influence attitudes. In 1933, Hitler made Goebbels the Minister of People's Enlightenment and Propaganda. In this role, Goebbels co-ordinated Nazi policy towards the media, sport, culture and the Arts, so that attitudes which Nazis opposed were censored and attitudes which Nazis supported were promoted by propaganda. For some, this made Joseph Goebbels the co-ordinator, or ringmaster, of attitudes in Nazi Germany.

Hitler had a simplistic view of propaganda. For him, it was just a matter of constantly repeating the Nazi message. For Goebbels, it was more complex. He wanted

Nazi attitudes to be so deeply buried in his propaganda that people did not even know that their attitudes were being changed (see Source C).

Source A

Joseph Goebbels speaking at a Nazi rally in 1938.

Source B

Hitler writing in *Mein Kampf* in 1925.

The purpose of propaganda is to convince the masses. Their slowness of understanding needs time to absorb information. Only constant repetition will finally succeed in imprinting an idea on the mind.

Source C

Goebbels explaining the use of propaganda.

The finest kind of propaganda does not reveal itself. The best propaganda is that which works invisibly, penetrating every cell of life in such a way that the public has no idea of the aims of the propagandist.

Activities ?

1 Write a sentence explaining why the Nazis used propaganda.

2 Using pages 92-98, write a paragraph explaining the different types of propaganda the Nazis used.

3 Which do you think would have been the most persuasive to the German people? Why?

Extend your knowledge

Joseph Goebbels

Joseph Goebbels was not a typical Nazi leader. He had not fought in the First World War, for example. He was short and had a club foot, which hindered his walking. He was an academic and had gained a doctorate in philosophy from Heidelberg University in 1920. He was outraged by what he saw as the mistreatment of Germany in the Treaty of Versailles in 1919.

Goebbels joined the Nazi Party in 1922. At first, he was not an admirer of Hitler. However, at the Bamberg Conference of 1926, Hitler won him over and Goebbels became a close ally.

In 1930, Goebbels became the Nazi Party's Head of Propaganda. He co-ordinated Hitler's campaigns for the presidency in 1932 and the Nazi Party general election campaigns.

When the Nazis came to power in Germany, Goebbels was Minister for People's Enlightenment and Propaganda. As well as being a superb organiser, he was an able speaker, presenting Nazi policy at rallies and on the radio.

Nazi use of the media

The press

Newspapers flourished under the Nazis – but they had to provide views with which the Ministry agreed, or face the consequences.

- Journalists were sometimes told what they could not publish. This was censorship (see Source D).
- They were also given regular briefings, containing the information the government were willing to release and they were sometimes given direct instructions what to write. This was propaganda (see Source E).

Any newspapers which opposed Nazi views were closed down. 1,600 newspapers were closed down in 1935 alone. This meant that there was no real free press in Germany – every newspaper was a Nazi newspaper.

Source D

Ministry of Propaganda order, 1935.

Photos showing Reich government ministers at dining tables with rows of bottles must not be published in future. This has given the absurd impression that members of the government are living it up.

Source E

General Instruction No. 674, given to the press in September 1939 by the Ministry of Public Enlightenment and Propaganda.

In the next issue, there must be a lead article, featured as prominently as possible, in which the decision of the Führer, no matter what it may be, will be discussed as the only possible one for Germany.

Exam-style question, Section A

Study Source F.

Give **two** things you can infer from Source F about Nazi propaganda.   **4 marks**

Radio

In the 1920s and early 1930s, Goebbels had already started to use the power of the radio in Nazi election campaigns. After 1933, he censored radio stations and used them to broadcast Nazi propaganda.

- All radio stations were put under Nazi control.
- Hitler and other Nazi officials made frequent broadcasts (see Source F).
- Cheap mass-produced radios were sold to the public. They were also placed in cafes, factories and schools. Speakers were even placed in the street. By 1939, 70% of German homes had a radio – more than anywhere else in Europe.
- All radios had to be designed to have a short range, so that they could not pick up foreign stations.

Exam tip

This question tests source analysis, specifically the skill of making inferences.

A good answer will work out what can be inferred about Nazi propaganda using selected details in the source – e.g. *"speaking on all German radio stations"*.

Source F

Ministry of Propaganda order, March 1934.

Attention! On Wednesday 21 March, the Führer is speaking on all German [radio] stations from 11 a.m. to 11.50 a.m... All factory owners, stores, offices, shops, pubs and flats must put up speakers an hour before, so that the whole workforce can hear.

Nazi use of rallies

Goebbels had used mass rallies and parades in election campaigns for the Nazis in the 1920s and early 1930s. Now that he had the entire resources of the German state at his disposal, he made Nazi rallies and parades bigger and more frequent. For example, a mass rally was held each year at Nuremberg, to create a sense of German unity and advertise the strength of the Nazi Party and Nazi Germany. At the 1934 Nuremburg rally, the stadium had a giant eagle with a 100-foot wing-spread, as well as thousands of swastika banners. It was surrounded by 130 anti-aircraft searchlights with a range of 25,000 feet, shining into the sky and forming walls of light around a crowd of 200,000 party supporters waving 20,000 flags.

Nazi use of sport

Goebbels also used sport to influence attitudes and increase support for the Nazi Party and Nazi attitudes (see Source G). He did this by 'Nazifying' sport. This meant:

- covering sports stadiums with Nazi symbols, linking enthusiasm for sports with enthusiasm for Nazism
- insisting that all teams – including visiting teams from abroad – make the Nazi straight-armed salute during the German national anthem, so that sports stars seemed to be paying respect to the Nazi state
- hailing sports victories as victories for Nazi ideals, such as striving to be the best.

The Berlin Olympics of 1936

Hitler's best opportunity to use sport as propaganda and to show Nazi Germany in a good light was in 1936, when the Olympic Games were held in Berlin.

- The Nazis built an Olympic stadium which could hold 110,000 people – the largest stadium in the world. It was decked out with swastikas and other Nazi symbols.
- All the events were very well organised, to demonstrate Nazi efficiency.
- Germany won 33 medals – more than any other country. Goebbels hailed this as a success for Nazism.
- The games were filmed by one of Germany's leading film directors, Leni Riefenstahl. She released two films in 1938, both of which were used for Nazi propaganda.
- There was also an element of censorship. The Reich Press Chamber issued an order that, if the press printed any information about the Olympics before the official press report, it was 'at their own risk'.

Source G

A statement by Joseph Goebbels in April 1933.

```
German sport has only one
task: to strengthen the
character of the German
people, imbuing it with
the fighting spirit and
comradeship needed in the
struggle for existence.
```

Activities

1 Make a table with two columns, headed 'Censorship' and 'Propaganda'. In the columns, list all the ways the Nazis attempted to control – by censorship, influence or propaganda – the attitudes of the German people.

2 In a class discussion, try to clarify what 'Nazification of Germany' means. Include in your discussion examples of Nazi treatment of religion, sport and the legal system.

Source H

A photograph of German football fans giving the Nazi salute during an international match against England, December 1935.

Nazi control of culture and the Arts

The Nazis had strong objections to many modern aspects of modern culture which had emerged during the Weimar Republic (see pages 36–38 for details). Instead, they favoured cultural activities, which stressed:

- romantic ideas about Germany's past, such as country life and strong families
- Nazi ideals, like loyalty, struggle, self-sacrifice and discipline.

So, in September 1933, they set up the Reich Chamber of Culture, which covered art and architecture, literature, music, theatre and film. It was overseen by Joseph Goebbels and the Ministry of Propaganda. The role of the Chamber of Culture was to make sure that cultural activities in Germany were *consistent* with Nazi ideas. They called this idea of consistency *Gleichschaltung* (see Interpretation 1). The Chamber of Culture banned cultural activity with which they disagreed and promoted culture which fitted Nazi beliefs.

Interpretation 1

From the website of the US Holocaust Memorial Museum, opened in 1993 to record details of the treatment of Jews by Nazi Germany.

One of the first tasks Nazi leaders undertook when they came to power in early 1933 was the synchronization (*Gleichschaltung*) of all professional and social organizations with Nazi ideology and policy. The arts and cultural organizations were not exempt from this effort. Joseph Goebbels, the Minister for Popular Enlightenment and Propaganda, immediately strove to bring the artistic and cultural communities in line with Nazi goals.

Art in Nazi Germany

Under the Chamber of Culture, the Nazis set up a Reich Chamber of Visual Arts. All painters and sculptors in Germany were required to apply to be members. 42,000 artists were accepted. Any artists who were refused membership or had their membership taken away were forbidden to teach, produce or sell art (see Source I).

Source I

From an official Nazi government letter to a German artist. Six hundred and eight of his paintings were also confiscated.

```
I hereby expel you from the National Chamber
of Fine Arts and forbid you, effective
immediately, any activity, professional or
amateur, in the field of graphic arts.
```

In 1936, over 12,000 paintings and sculptures were removed from art galleries. The pieces of art included work by famous artists such as Picasso, Cézanne and Van Gogh. The Gestapo made surprise visits to artists' studios to check that Chamber of Fine Arts rules were not broken.

To encourage the kind of art which the Nazis did approve of, art competitions were held, with large prizes for the winners. The Greater German Art Exhibition, including 900 exhibits, was held in 1936.

Source J

A painting called *The Führer Speaks*, by Paul Padua, produced in 1939. It shows a family listening to a radio broadcast by Hitler.

Architecture in Nazi Germany

The Nazis also had strong ideas about architecture. They disliked the 'modernist' and 'futuristic' architecture of the Weimar Republic in the 1920s (see page 37 in Chapter 1). They wanted buildings which made Nazi Germany seem powerful.

The architect who became a personal favourite of Hitler, who designed many of Nazi Germany's major buildings, was Albert Speer. His major projects were:

- the parade ground for the Nazi rallies in Nuremberg in 1934
- the new Chancellery – the offices of the Chancellor – in Berlin in 1938.

Speer used design features which shaped people's impressions of Germany and the Nazi Party.

- He built huge buildings, so that size gave the impression of power and permanence.
- He also used features from Ancient Rome and Ancient Greece, such as domes, arches and pillars, so that the buildings seemed grand and historic.
- He decorated his buildings with massive Nazi flags. This was partly for artistic effect, but it was also so that the powerful impact of the buildings reflected on the Nazi Party.

Music in Nazi Germany

The Nazis also tried to control the performance and composition of music in Germany. Some types of music were censored. For example, jazz music was banned, as it was seen as the work of black people and therefore inferior. The work of Mendelssohn was also banned, because he was partly Jewish.

Some music, on the other hand, was promoted, because it emphasised aspects of German culture which the Nazis liked. For example:

- Richard Wagner was favoured because he put to music the legends of heroic and powerful Germans from the past.
- Beethoven, Bach and traditional German folk music were also favoured.

Source K

A photograph of a building designed by Albert Speer for the Nazi Party rallies at Nuremberg, taken in 1938.

96

Literature in Nazi Germany

The Nazis also had strong ideas about literature and which books should be available to the German people.

- No new books could be published without approval from The Chamber of Culture.
- Existing books containing views which the Nazis didn't like were censored. 2,500 writers were officially banned.
- Millions of books were taken from universities and public libraries and burned on huge, public bonfires. In May 1933, students in Berlin burned 20,000 books written by Jews, communists and anti-Nazi authors, destroying books, by Sigmund Freud and Albert Einstein, amongst others (see Source L).

Source M

A photograph of Nazi supporters burning books in Berlin on 10 May 1933.

Source L

Extracts from the 'Twelve Theses against the Un-German Spirit', which set out guidelines to German university students on banned literature. These guidelines were posted around German universities in May, 1933.

```
1. It is the German Volk's
[people's] responsibility
to assure that its language
and literature are the
pure expression of its
traditions.

2. At present there is
a chasm [gap] between
literature and German
tradition. This situation is
a disgrace.

4. Our most dangerous enemy
is the Jew and those who are
his slaves.

5. A Jew can only think
Jewish. If he writes in
German, he is lying. The
German who writes in German,
but thinks un-German, is a
traitor!
```

Film in Nazi Germany

Goebbels also exerted control over the German film industry and tried to make sure that films supported Nazi ideas. With audiences of over 250 million in 1933, cinemas were useful for getting Nazi views across.

- Films shown in cinemas were preceded by a 45-minute official newsreel, publicising Germany's achievements.
- All film-makers had to send plot details of every new film to Goebbels for approval.

- The Nazi Party also made its own films for general release. In total, they made about 1,300 films.
- Some Nazi films were for entertainment – but they had underlying political messages, such as *Hitlerjunge Quex* (1933), in which a young member of the Nazi Party is killed by communists.
- Some Nazi films were more obvious propaganda. Goebbels had a propaganda cartoon made for cinemas, with a leading character, Hansi the canary, based on Mickey Mouse. Hansi had a lick of hair across his forehead, just like Hitler. In the film, Hansi is pestered by villainous black crows with stereotypical Jewish features.

Activities

1 Continue the table you started on page 94.

   a Under the heading 'Censorship', list all the ways in which the Nazis banned cultural activity they didn't like.

   b Under the heading 'Propaganda', list the ways they used culture to promote Nazi ideas and attitudes.

2 Look at Source J on page 95. Why do you think the Nazi Party would have approved of it?

3 Working as a whole class, look at pages 95–97 and agree two or three sentences which explain what *Gleichschaltung* means.

Summary

- In Nazi Germany, censorship and propaganda were used to control and influence attitudes.
- Joseph Goebbels, head of the Ministry of People's Enlightenment and Propaganda, was the co-ordinator of Nazi censorship and propaganda.
- Nazi control and influence of attitudes was exerted using the media, rallies and sport, including the Olympic Games.
- The Nazis also exerted control over the Arts, including art, architecture, literature and film.

Checkpoint

Strengthen

S1 Explain what the terms censorship and propaganda mean.

S2 Describe the role of Joseph Goebbels and the Ministry of People's Enlightenment and Propaganda.

S3 How did the Nazis use the press and radio to influence attitudes?

S4 How did the Nazis use rallies for propaganda?

S5 How did the Nazis use sport to influence attitudes in Germany?

S6 Describe how the Nazis controlled the Arts, including art, architecture, literature and film.

Challenge

C1 Weigh up how far the Nazis influenced attitudes in Germany by compulsion (e.g. censorship) and how far they influenced attitudes by persuasion (e.g. propaganda).

C2 Explain, with detailed examples, the Nazi policy of *Gleichschaltung*.

How confident do you feel about your answers to these questions? If you are unsure, look again at pages 91–92 for S1 and S2, page 93 for S3 and S4, page 94 for S5 and 95–97 for S6; for C1 and C2, join together with others and discuss a joint answer. Your teacher can provide hints.

3.4 Opposition, resistance and conformity

Learning outcomes

- Understand the different groups of people who resisted the Nazis, including resistance from the Church and young people.

Support for the Nazi regime

There was a high level of support amongst German people for Hitler and the Nazis. Hitler won 36% of the vote in the April 1932 presidential election, and then the Nazi Party won 38% of votes in the July 1932 general election. The Nazis were elected as the largest party in the Reichstag. For the rest of the 1930s, amongst most Germans there was a high level of **conformity**, or acceptance, of Hitler and the Nazis and their policies.

- One reason was censorship and propaganda. Joseph Goebbels banned criticism of the Nazis and used the media to spread positive messages about them, ensuring that Hitler and the Nazis remained popular in Germany.

- Another reason was Nazi success. For example, during the 1930s, Hitler reduced unemployment and achieved several successes in foreign policy.

As a result, conformity and support for Hitler and the Nazis was very strong (see Source A).

However, there were several areas of opposition to the Nazis, shown in Figure 3.2.

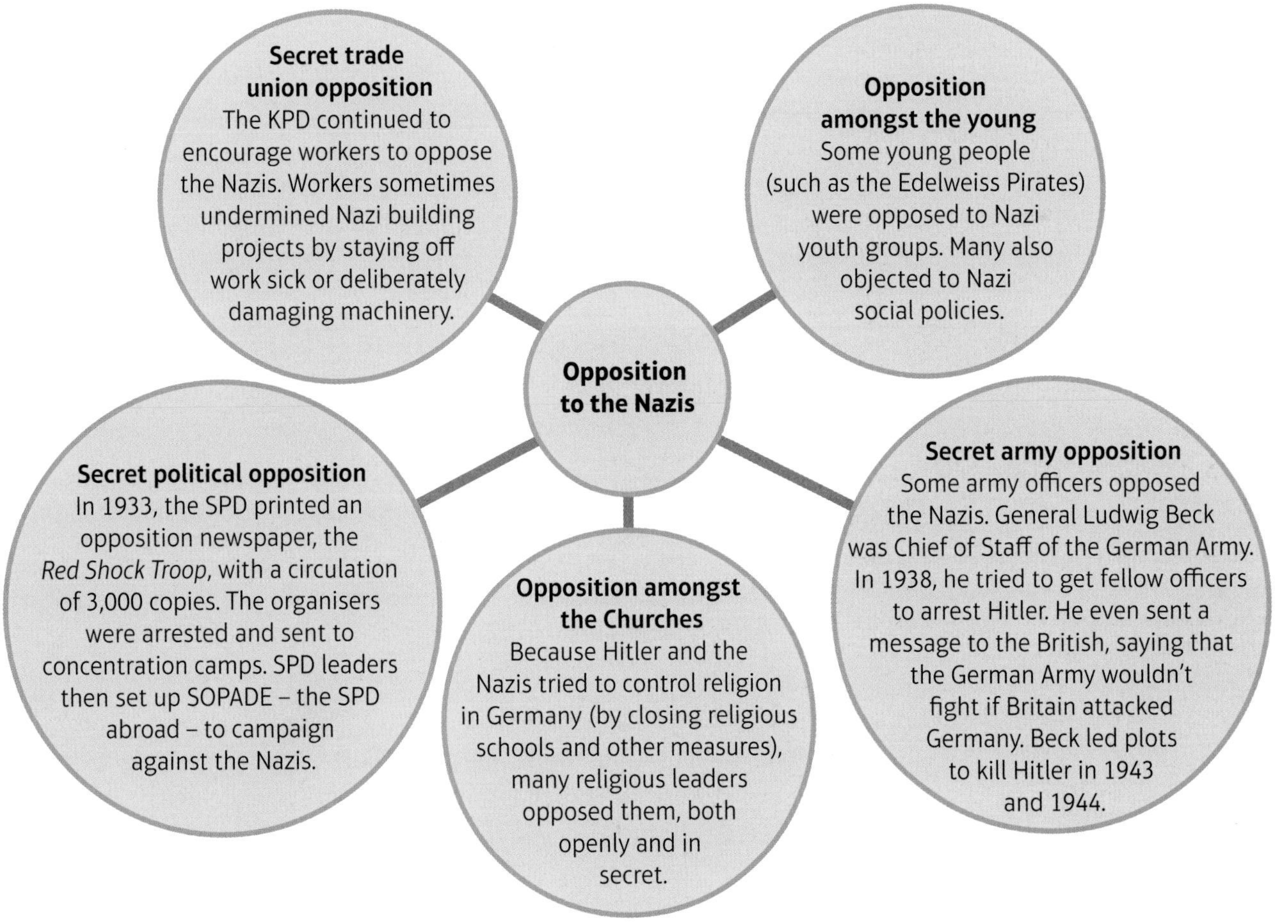

Secret trade union opposition
The KPD continued to encourage workers to oppose the Nazis. Workers sometimes undermined Nazi building projects by staying off work sick or deliberately damaging machinery.

Opposition amongst the young
Some young people (such as the Edelweiss Pirates) were opposed to Nazi youth groups. Many also objected to Nazi social policies.

Opposition to the Nazis

Secret political opposition
In 1933, the SPD printed an opposition newspaper, the *Red Shock Troop*, with a circulation of 3,000 copies. The organisers were arrested and sent to concentration camps. SPD leaders then set up SOPADE – the SPD abroad – to campaign against the Nazis.

Opposition amongst the Churches
Because Hitler and the Nazis tried to control religion in Germany (by closing religious schools and other measures), many religious leaders opposed them, both openly and in secret.

Secret army opposition
Some army officers opposed the Nazis. General Ludwig Beck was Chief of Staff of the German Army. In 1938, he tried to get fellow officers to arrest Hitler. He even sent a message to the British, saying that the German Army wouldn't fight if Britain attacked Germany. Beck led plots to kill Hitler in 1943 and 1944.

Figure 3.2 Opposition to Hitler and the Nazis.

From a speech by David Lloyd George, an ex-prime minister of Britain, speaking to the British press in 1937.

Whatever one may think of his (Hitler's) methods... there can be no doubt that he has achieved a marvellous transformation in the spirit of the people... and in their social and economic outlook... As to his popularity, especially among the youth of Germany, there can be no manner of doubt. The old trust him; the young idolise him. It is not the admiration accorded to a popular leader. It is the worship of a national hero who has saved his country from utter despondency and degradation.

Resistance and opposition

There was some resistance and opposition to the Nazis. **Resistance** means refusing to support something or speaking against it. **Opposition** means actively working against something in order to remove it. For example, some Germans disagreed with the banning of political parties and trade unions, and the persecution of Jews; some even spoke out against it. However, few people actually opposed the Nazis and tried to stop them.

It is hard to know how much opposition there was to Hitler and the Nazis. There are various reasons for this.

- Organised opposition, in the form of political parties or trade unions, was banned.
- Unofficial opposition was risky. Criticism of Hitler was reported to the Gestapo by informers and those reported would be punished.

Perhaps it is remarkable that there was *any* resistance and opposition to the Nazis at all. But there was.

Opposition from churches

Hitler and the Nazis tried to control religion in Germany (see pages 88–89).

- Catholic bishops had to swear allegiance to the Nazi Regime; Catholic schools and Catholic youth groups were closed.
- Protestant pastors were told to join the German Christian Church, which accepted Nazi interference in the running of Protestant churches. Nazis called it The Reich (or state) Church. Many pastors conformed, but some Christian leaders resisted.

The Pastors' Emergency League (PEL)

In 1933, a group of Protestant pastors, including Martin Niemöller, set up the Pastors' Emergency League (PEL). They opposed two key aspects of Nazi treatment of Protestant Churches in Germany.

1 The joining of regional churches into one national German Christian Church.

2 Nazi attempts to stop Jews becoming Christians and to ban the Jewish Old Testament from Christian teaching.

The Confessing Church

In 1934, the PEL set up the Confessing Church. This meant, in effect, there were two Protestant Churches in Germany. One was the Reich Church, which accepted Nazi interference in the running of their Church. The other, the Confessing Church, opposed Nazi interference. About 2,000 Protestant pastors remained in the German Christian Church, but about 6,000 joined the Confessing Church, in opposition to Nazi policy. Some pastors spoke out against the Nazis. About 800 were arrested and sent to concentration camps.

Catholic opposition

Some Catholic priests also spoke out against Nazi ideas and policies. Around 400 Catholic priests were eventually imprisoned in the Priests' Block at Dachau concentration camp.

The limits of Church opposition

Though many Church leaders did voice opposition to the Nazis, their opposition was limited (see Interpretation 1). Opposition to the Nazis amongst ordinary Christians was also muted. There were big attendances at church services, in defiance of the Nazis. Some Germans even publicly applauded Church leaders who opposed the Nazis. These are examples of a refusal to conform – a kind of resistance to the Nazis. But there were few Christians who were brave, or foolish enough to oppose the Nazis openly.

Interpretation 1

From *The Nazi Dictatorship*, by Ian Kershaw published in 1985.

The Churches offered less than fundamental resistance to Nazism. Their energies were used in opposing Nazi interference with their traditional practices. This was not matched by equally vigorous denunciation of Nazi inhumanity and barbarism.

The role of Pastor Martin Niemöller

During the First World War, Martin Niemöller had been a German U-Boat (submarine) commander. He trained as a pastor in 1920 and later became a key opponent of the Nazis. But he wasn't *completely* against them.

In the 1920s, Niemöller opposed the Weimar Republic. He thought Germany needed a strong leader. He voted for the Nazis in the 1924 and 1933 elections and welcomed Hitler's appointment as Chancellor in 1933.

- However, he opposed Nazi interference in the running of the Protestant Church in Germany. He was a founder of the PEL in 1933 and the Confessing Church in 1934.
- Niemöller also opposed the Nazi ban on Jews becoming Christians – although he did not oppose other restrictions on Jews which the Nazis imposed in the 1930s.

In 1934, Niemöller discovered that, as a critic of the Nazis, his telephone had been bugged by the Gestapo. He began to realise that the Nazi regime was a dictatorship which should be opposed. He spoke out against them more and more, opposing their policies. As a result, he was repeatedly arrested between 1934 and 1937.

In 1937, he was arrested by the Gestapo and charged with 'treasonable statements' – statements which opposed the Nazi state. He was found guilty in 1938 and imprisoned, in solitary confinement, in Sachsenhausen concentration camp.

Niemöller continued to have mixed feelings about the Nazis. In 1939, he even asked if he could be released from prison to fight for Germany in the Second World War, offering to serve Hitler 'in any capacity'.

He was later transferred to Dachau concentration camp, where he remained until the end of the war in 1945, when he was freed.

Source B

A lesson used frequently by Martin Niemöller in sermons and speeches. He used it to condemn Church leaders who did little to speak out against the evils of Nazi Germany in the 1930s.

```
First they came for the Socialists, and I did
not speak out—because I was not a Socialist.

Then they came for the Trade Unionists, and
I did not speak out—because I was not a
Trade Unionist.

Then they came for the Jews, and I did not
speak out—because I was not a Jew.

Then they came for me—and there was no one
left to speak for me.
```

Activities ?

1. Make a table with two columns. In one column, list ways Christian Churches in Germany resisted or opposed Hitler and the Nazis. In the other column, list ways in which they didn't.
2. Make a similar table for Martin Neimöller, to show his opposition and support for the Nazis.
3. Use your two tables to answer the following question: Interpretation 1 says religious opposition to the Nazis was limited. How far do you agree?

Opposition from the young

In the 1920s, Hitler had developed sections of the Nazi Party especially for young people, such as the Hitler Youth and League of German Girls (see page 56). After he became Chancellor, Hitler expanded the Nazi youth programme. Eventually, all young people were expected to attend (see pages 115–118).

Most young Germans conformed, but some young people were opposed to these Nazi youth groups.

Source C

A young man describing the activities and atmosphere at a Hitler Youth camp in 1938.

We hardly had any free time. Everything was done in a military way, from reveille (early morning bugle call), first parade, raising the flag, morning sport and ablutions, through breakfast to the 'scouting games', lunch and so on into the evening. Several participants left the camp because the whole slog was too stupid for them... Comradeship was very poor, and everything was done for command and obedience.

Some German youngsters also objected to Nazi social policies. For the Nazis, everything – including industry, agriculture and education – was organised for the benefit of the state. People had no freedom of choice. This put off some young people, especially if they were rebellious. As a result, alternative youth groups grew up in defiance of the official Nazi groups. The best known were the Edelweiss Pirates and the Swing Youth.

The Edelweiss Pirates

The Edelweiss Pirates emerged in the late 1930s in working-class districts of big German cities.

Local groups called themselves the 'Travelling Dudes' from Essen or the 'Navajos' in Cologne. They used the symbol of the white edelweiss flower to show their allegiance to the Edelweiss Pirates.

The Pirates consisted of teenagers – both boys and girls, but mainly boys – who resented the military discipline of the Nazi youth groups and the general lack of freedom in Nazi Germany. Stressing their own freedom to choose, the boys wore their hair longer and copied styles of clothing they saw in America, often opting for white or checked shirts and white socks.

In the cities, they hung around on street corners where they were difficult for the Gestapo to distinguish from any other young people. If they came across any Hitler Youth, they would taunt them or sometimes even attack them. To break away from adults and Nazi restrictions, the Pirates went on long hikes in the countryside. They pitched tents, sang parodies of Hitler Youth songs and told jokes, sometimes mocking the Nazis.

Source D

A photograph of Edelweiss Pirates from 1938.

The Swing Youth

The Swing Youth were mainly teenagers from the wealthy middle-class families, located in big towns, especially Berlin, Hamburg and Kiel. They admired American culture, such as American clothes, films and especially music.

Because they were from wealthier families, the Swing Youth often owned record players and played records illegally imported from America. Their favourites were the swing bands like the Glen Miller Orchestra. They liked to gather together, usually drinking alcohol and smoking, to listen and dance in groups; a favourite dance was the 'jitterbug'. Gradually, they began to organise illegal dances. These were attended by up to 6,000 young people.

Some youngsters preferred a different type of American music – jazz – made popular by black singers and musicians such as Louis Armstrong. German followers of jazz were called the Jazz Youth. Heinrich Himmler, the leader of the SS said that any young people who listened to jazz music should be 'beaten, given the severest exercise and then put to hard labour'.

Source E

From a report on the Swing Youth in 1939, carried out in 1944 by the Nazi Reich Ministry of Justice.

```
At the turn of 1939-40, the Flottbeck group
(of Swing Youth) organised dances which were
attended by 5,000 to 6,000 people and they
were marked by an uninhibited indulgence
in swing... They regard Englishmen as the
highest form of human development. A false
conception of freedom leads them into
opposition to the Hitler Youth.
```

Opposition or resistance?

Up to 1939, the opposition of the Edelweiss Pirates and the Swing Youth to the Nazis was limited.

- Their actions were limited. The Pirates and the Swing Youth resisted Nazi expectations but, apart from occasionally daubing anti-Nazi graffiti, telling anti-Nazi jokes and attacking members of Hitler Youth, they did little to oppose the Nazis. It was only after 1939, when the Second World War disrupted German society, that some Edelweiss Pirates began to make physical attacks against the government.

- Their motives were limited. The opposition of these alternative youth groups to the Nazis was mainly cultural – concerned with clothes, music and behaviour – rather than political. The Pirates and the Swing Youth wanted freedom from Nazi controls, but they were not a political opposition.

- Their numbers were limited. By 1939, membership of the Edelweiss Pirates was about 2,000. Membership of Hitler Youth by that date was about eight million.

The existence of these alternative youth groups shows that a minority of German youth remained unconvinced by Nazi expectations and were opposed enough to defy Nazi expectations. However, it cannot be said that the Edelweiss Pirates or Swing Youth were typical of German youth – and they certainly were not the kind of opposition to the Nazis that posed any threat to Hitler's Germany.

Extend your knowledge

Edelweiss Pirates

Search online for images of the Edelweiss Pirates. Then search for images of Hitler Youth. What similarities are there between the two groups? What differences are there?

Activities ?

1 List three reasons why some young Germans preferred to set up their own youth groups rather than attend Hitler Youth or the League of German Girls.

2 Work in pairs. One person should create a one-minute speech about the Edelweiss Pirates; the other a one-minute speech on the Swing Youth. After giving your speeches, both write a paragraph recording the key points about each group.

3 Look back at pages 99–103 and recall that **conformity** is going along with something, **resistance** is going against it, and **opposition** is trying to destroy it.

   a As a whole class, discuss how much conformity, resistance and opposition to Hitler and the Nazis there was amongst people in Germany in the 1930s.

   b Make your own judgement, then write one side of A4 to explain and justify your opinion.

Exam-style question, Section A

Explain why there was so little resistance and opposition to Hitler and the Nazis in Germany in the years 1933–39.

You may use the following in your answer:

* Nazi propaganda
* The Gestapo.

You **must** also use information of your own.   **12 marks**

Exam tip

A good answer will:

* include at least three factors which were reasons why there was so little resistance and opposition to Hitler and the Nazis
* have detailed information about how each reason restricted resistance and opposition.

Summary

* Most Germans supported Hitler and the Nazis, or at least conformed to Nazi expectations.
* Resistance and opposition were limited because of Nazi propaganda and the Nazi police state, which prevented criticism of the Nazis, and because of Nazi successes in areas such as foreign policy and employment.
* However, there was some resistance and opposition.
* Opposition came from elements amongst political groups, trade unions, the army, the Churches and youth groups.
* Some Church leaders opposed the Nazis, but they were in a minority and were punished.
* Some young people set up alternatives to Nazi youth groups, but, although they defied the Nazis, they never really opposed them before 1939.
* Those who disapproved of the Nazis resisted Nazi expectations and sometimes voiced disapproval, but very few people were brave enough to oppose Hitler and the Nazis openly.

Checkpoint

Strengthen

S1 Explain what conformity, resistance and opposition are.

S2 Describe the support and conformity the Nazis enjoyed in the 1930s.

S3 Describe the opposition to the Nazis amongst political groups, trade unions and the army.

S4 What opposition was there against the Nazis by Church leaders?

S5 What opposition was there against the Nazis by German youth groups?

Challenge

C1 Weigh up the relative amounts of support, conformity, resistance and opposition to Hitler and the Nazis in the 1930s.

C2 Explain why the amount of resistance and opposition was so limited.

How confident do you feel about your answers to these questions? If you are unsure, look again at page 99 for S1–S3, pages 100–101 for S4 and pages 102–103 for S5; for C1 and C2, join together with others who want to consider the same question and discuss a joint answer. Your teacher can provide hints.

Recap: Nazi control and dictatorship, 1933–39

Recall quiz

1 When was the Reichstag Fire?
2 When was the Enabling Act?
3 When was the Night of the Long Knives?
4 Who was Hitler's head of the SS?
5 Name the Nazi leader who was put in charge of the SD and the Gestapo.
6 Who was Hitler's Minister of Propaganda?
7 What was the Nazi policy of *Gleichschaltung*?

8 Who was the U-boat commander, and later a Protestant pastor, who became a key critic of Nazi religious policies?
9 What was the name of the youth group which set up in opposition to the Hitler Youth and which used a white flower as its emblem?
10 What was the name given to the youth movement of young Germans who met to listen and dance to American big band music?

Activities

1 Write a paragraph to explain why the Reichstag Fire was important.
2 List three ways that the Enabling Act changed how laws were made in Germany. What was the effect of these changes?
3 On a sheet of A4 paper, make a diagram called 'Controlling Nazi Germany'. Draw a large set of weighing scales at the bottom of the page.

    a On one side of the weighing scales, list all the ways in which the Nazis controlled Nazi Germany by force – e.g. by police activity, by punishments or by banning things.

    b On the other side of the weighing scales, list all the ways in which the Nazis controlled Nazi Germany by persuasion – e.g. by propaganda or by agreements.

4 What were the key differences between the Arts in the Weimar Republic and the Arts in Nazi Germany?
5 Look at the diagram on page 99 showing opposition to Hitler and the Nazis. Copy the diagram onto a sheet of A4 paper. Use the information on pages 100–103 to put brief details in the text boxes on 'Opposition amongst the churches' and 'Opposition amongst the young'.

Exam-style question, Section A

Explain why Hitler was able to increase his control over Germany between 1933 and 1939.

You may use the following in your answer:

- the Enabling Act
- Nazi propaganda.

You **must** also use information of your own.　**12 marks**

Exam tip

A good answer will:

- include at least three factors which were reasons why Hitler was able to increase his control over Germany
- have detailed information about how each reason increased his control of Germany.

Writing historically: explaining and evaluating

Think about the purpose of your writing to help structure it and choose how you express your ideas.

Learning outcomes

By the end of this lesson, you will understand how to:

- use the key features of explanatory and analytical writing
- structure your writing to ensure you explain or evaluate effectively.

Definitions

Explain: to make an idea clear using relevant facts, details and examples.

Evaluate: to examine two or more points of view closely and carefully in order to make a judgement or come to a conclusion.

What are the similarities and differences in writing to **explain** and writing to **evaluate**?

Compare these two exam-style questions (note Question B has been adapted to make reference to Interpretation 2):

Question A

Explain why there was so little resistance and opposition to Hitler and the Nazis in Germany in the years 1933–39. **(12 marks)**

Question B

How far do you agree with Interpretation 1 (see page 136) about the events of *Kristallnacht* in 1938?

Explain your answer using Interpretations 1 and 2 (see page 136) and your knowledge of the historical context. **(16 marks)**

1. Look at the statements below. Which apply to Question A, which to Question B and which to both? This type of question:

   a. asks you to write to explain.

   b. asks you to evaluate.

   c. asks you to consider arguments for and against a point of view and reach a conclusion.

   d. requires you to explain how and why an event happened or a situation came about.

   e. requires you to provide evidence and examples to support your ideas.

   f. requires you to link all your ideas to key points.

   g. requires you to consider what contributed to a situation or event.

   h. requires you to link and develop your ideas logically to form a line of reasoning.

   i. requires you to demonstrate good knowledge and understanding of the features or characteristics of the historical period.

   j. requires you to explore how and why a series of circumstances, events or actions led to a particular outcome.

2. Look at your answers to Question 1. What are the key differences between questions that ask you to 'explain' and questions that ask you 'how far do you agree'?

How can I structure writing to explain and writing to evaluate?

3. Answers to explain why questions often follow the structure: 1st point; 2nd point; 3rd point; Summary of causes and effects that led to a specific outcome.

The start of some sentences have been written out below in answer to Question A. Put the sentences in the order in which you think they should appear.

a. Once Hitler had the power to pass laws without consulting the Reichstag, he set about removing other sources of opposition.

b. Goebbels's use of propaganda was important because...

c. Although there was some resistance, particularly in youth groups, Hitler managed to gain a lot of German support from 1933...

d. Hitler's control of culture and the Arts were another key reason for his success...

e. Hitler's decision to get rid of the SA was also significant...

4. Now look at the plan below for an answer to an exam-style question that asks you to evaluate. Remember, in the exam you would need to refer to both interpretations in the question.

1st point to support the interpretation	a. In 1933, before Kristallnacht, the brownshirts (SA) had helped to enforce the official boycott of Jewish businesses, which...
2nd point to support the interpretation	b. These boycotts were still happening in 1938. Across Germany, the brownshirts would stand outside shops with banners discouraging people entering...
Signal a turning point in the argument	c. However, Interpretation 1 does not take into account that many ordinary Germans did not actively take part in the destruction and violence...
1st point to contradict the interpretation	d. Many ordinary Germans were horrified by the destruction...
2nd point to contradict the interpretation	e. Opposition to Kristallnacht might not have been strong because people feared being arrested or killed...
Conclusion: a judgement directly responding to the interpretation	f. Interpretation 1 is correct in some things that is says, but I cannot agree with it fully because...

5. Look at these exam-style questions:

Explain why Germany experienced recovery between 1924 and 1929. **(12 marks)**

How far do you agree with Interpretation 1 (see page 136) about the events of *Kristallnacht* in 1938?

Explain your answer, using Interpretation 1 (on page 62) and Interpretation 3 (on page 64) and your knowledge of the historical context. **(16 marks)**

Plan an answer to each one, using the same structures as the responses above. Write the first sentence of each paragraph.

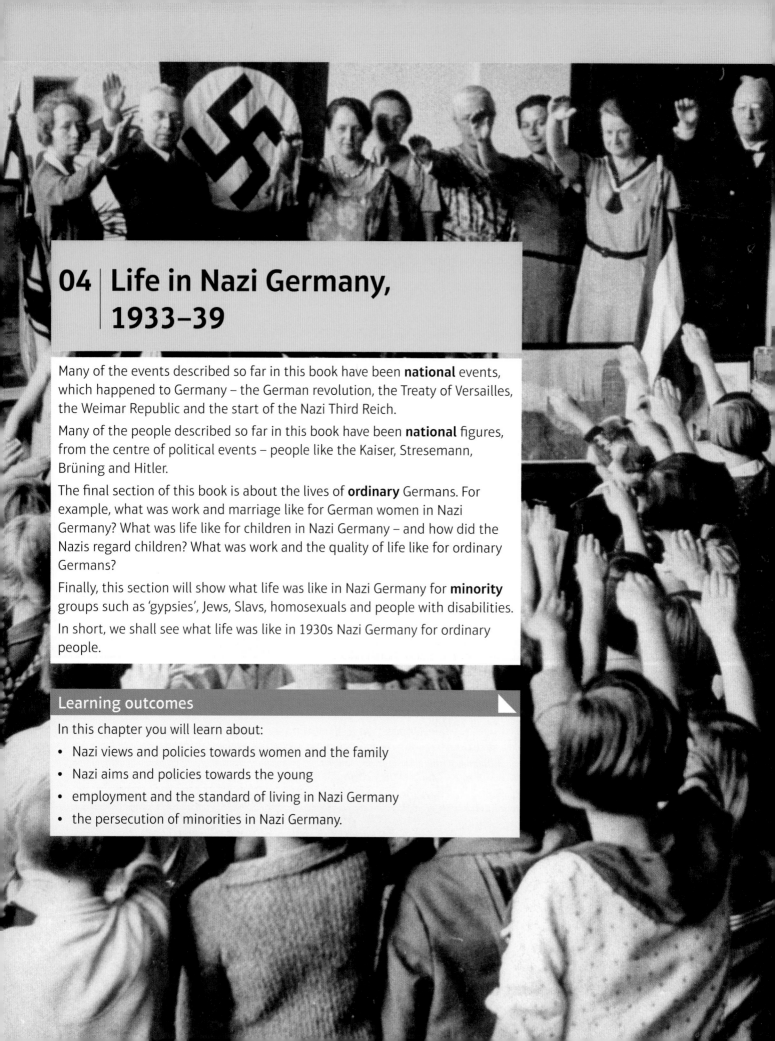

04 | Life in Nazi Germany, 1933–39

Many of the events described so far in this book have been **national** events, which happened to Germany – the German revolution, the Treaty of Versailles, the Weimar Republic and the start of the Nazi Third Reich.

Many of the people described so far in this book have been **national** figures, from the centre of political events – people like the Kaiser, Stresemann, Brüning and Hitler.

The final section of this book is about the lives of **ordinary** Germans. For example, what was work and marriage like for German women in Nazi Germany? What was life like for children in Nazi Germany – and how did the Nazis regard children? What was work and the quality of life like for ordinary Germans?

Finally, this section will show what life was like in Nazi Germany for **minority** groups such as 'gypsies', Jews, Slavs, homosexuals and people with disabilities.

In short, we shall see what life was like in 1930s Nazi Germany for ordinary people.

Learning outcomes

In this chapter you will learn about:

- Nazi views and policies towards women and the family
- Nazi aims and policies towards the young
- employment and the standard of living in Nazi Germany
- the persecution of minorities in Nazi Germany.

4.1 Nazi policies towards women

- Understand Nazi policies towards women, and how effective they were.

Chapter 1 showed what life was like for women in the Weimar Republic in the 1920s (see pages 34–35). This section is about what life was like for women under the Nazis in the 1930s..

Nazi views on women and the family

The Nazis believed that women should adopt the traditional role of mother and housewife, while the man provided for the family. Figure 4.1 shows the three main views the Nazis had about women and the family. However, Hitler did not portray women as unimportant – he described the role of women as equally as important as that of German men.

Source A

Joseph Goebbels, a leading Nazi, describing the role of women in 1929.

> The mission of women is to be beautiful and to bring children into the world. The female bird... hatches eggs for him. In exchange, the male takes care of gathering the food and stands guard and wards off the enemy.

Source B

Hitler, addressing a Nazi rally in Nuremberg in 1934.

> ... one might say that the world of a woman is a smaller world. For her world is her husband, her family, her children and her house. But where would the greater world be with no one to care for the small world? Every child that a woman brings into the world is a battle waged for the existence of her people.

Source C

A painting from 1939 by Adolf Wissel, an official Nazi artist, showing a German family.

Appearance: women should adopt a 'natural' look, with simple plaited or tied-back hair and long skirts.

Employment: The Nazis wanted women to stay at home rather than go to work, so they could raise a family. They believed that men were the main breadwinners, and that any woman in work could be taking a man's job. They disapproved of women in professions such as medicine and the law.

Marriage and family: birth rates should increase to make Germany bigger and stronger. The Nazis wanted women to marry and have as many children as possible. They believed that women should devote their lives to feeding and rearing their family. They stressed the importance of housecraft, skills like needlework and cookery.

Figure 4.1 Nazi views on women and the family.

Nazi Policies towards women

After the Nazis came into power in 1933, the Nazis could turn their ideas about women into policies which affected the lives of all women in Germany.

In 1934, the Nazis appointed a Reich Women's Leader, Gertrud Scholtz-Klink, to oversee all policies relating to women. She set about making German women servants of the German state and Hitler (see Source D).

Source D

A speech by Gertrud Scholtz-Klink, Reich Women's Leader, in 1936.

```
Not only will women with children become
mothers of the nation – but every German
woman and girl will become one of the
Führer's little helpers, wherever she is.
```

Scholtz-Klink insisted that all women's organisations would be forced to merge with a new Nazi organisation for women, called the German Women's Enterprise (*Deutsches Frauenwerk*, or DFW). If any organisations refused, they were banned. This gave the Nazis control of all the women's groups in Germany. Eventually, the German Women's Enterprise had six million members.

Through DFW activities, the Nazis could spread their ideas about women. For example, by 1939, 1.7 million women had attended Nazi courses on subjects such as childcare, cooking and sewing.

Women, marriage and the family

The birth rate was falling in Germany. In 1900, there had been two million births per year in Germany. By 1933, this had fallen to one million. The Nazis were concerned – fewer children meant fewer German workers and soldiers later on. Therefore, Nazis wanted to reverse the fall in the birth rate. As a result, the Nazis made several changes to the law to encourage marriage, motherhood and childbirth.

The Law for the Encouragement of Marriage, 1933

Loans, worth up to 1,000 marks – about eight months' wages – were provided to encourage young couples to marry. This law also encouraged wives to stay at home and bring up children, as the loans were only available if the wife stopped work. It also encouraged childbirth.

For each child born into a family, a quarter of the loan was written off. So, if a family had four children, the loan would be completely paid off.

Divorce laws

In 1938, the Nazis changed the divorce laws to encourage childbirth. If a wife would not (or could not) have children, or had an abortion, this could be used as grounds for divorce by the husband.

The Mother's Cross

The Mother's Cross encouraged childbirth. It was an award given to women for the number of children they had: bronze for four or five children, silver for six or seven and gold for eight. These were given as medals.

The Hitler Youth were ordered to salute wearers of gold medals. Mothers of ten children were expected to name Hitler as the godfather of the tenth child and, if it was a boy, name him Adolf.

Source E

Wilhelmine Haferkamp, a mother from the industrial city of Oberhausen, interviewed in the 1980s. She is describing the benefits she received for having many children – she eventually gave birth to 10.

```
I got 30 marks per child from the Hitler
government and 20 marks from the city. That
was a lot of money. I sometimes got more
'child money' than my husband earned... I
was proud. When I got the gold [Mother's
Cross medal], there was a big celebration in
a school, where the mothers were all invited
for coffee and cake.
```

Lebensborn

The **Lebensborn** (Fountain of Life) programme was another policy to encourage childbirth. This was started in 1935 by the SS leader, Heinrich Himmler.

At first, the policy only provided nurseries and financial aid for women who had children with SS men. Later, it encouraged single women to breed with SS men. This was to create 'genetically pure' children for worthy German families. Between 1938 and 1941, one *Lebensborn* home alone helped over 540 mothers give birth.

Extend your knowledge

Changing people's behaviour

Governments that want to change people's behaviour can't always do it by force. For example, the Nazis could not force women to have more children – but they could influence people's behaviour by changing the law.

For example, as well as receiving marriage loans, women could also get monthly payments from the government to help with the cost of bringing up children.

From 1936, a woman could get 10 marks per month for her third and fourth children and 20 marks for the fifth child and any subsequent child. An average income for a working father in 1936 was 150 marks per month, though this was taxed at 20%.

So, if a couple had 10 children, this meant that the wife often 'earned' a bigger monthly income for having children than the husband earned at work.

Activities

?

1 List three Nazi beliefs about marriage and the family.
2 For each Nazi belief on your list, note down policies on pages 110–111 which put that Nazi belief into practice.

Women and employment

Once in power, the Nazis worked to reduce the number of women in work, as they believed a woman's place was in the home, raising a family.

One way the Nazis reduced the number of women in work was by propaganda – they tried to persuade women to behave differently. Nazi posters showed women as wives and mothers and Nazi speeches encouraged women to leave work and become housewives (see Sources A, B and C on page 109). They told women to concentrate on the 'three Ks' – *Kinder, Küche, Kirche* – children, kitchen and the church. Many German women were persuaded (see Source F).

Source F

From an interview with Gertrud Draber in 2001, in which she is remembering what it was like to be a young woman in Nazi Germany.

Young girls from the age of ten onward were taught... to take care of their bodies, so they could bear as many children as the state needed... Birth control information is frowned on and practically forbidden.

My main aim as a woman was above all to become a mother. I wanted to be a perfect housewife. I wanted to do something different with my life, not just be a working girl in an office.

The Nazis also introduced new policies to reduce the number of women at work.

- From 1933, women were banned from professional posts as teachers, doctors and civil servants. By the end of 1934, about 360,000 women had given up work.
- From 1936, no women could become a judge or a lawyer, or even do jury service.
- Schoolgirls were trained for motherhood, not work. For example, they were taught housework, such as ironing, and other domestic tasks (see Source G).
- In 1937, grammar schools for girls, which prepared girls for university, were banned. The number of female students starting higher education fell from just over 17,000 in 1932 to 6,000 in 1939.

Source G

A photograph of girls in the League of German Girls from the 1930s, practising their domestic skills in preparation for motherhood.

The appearance of women in Nazi Germany

The Nazis never forced women to look a certain way through legislation. However, Nazi propaganda did (see Source C on page 109). Women were encouraged to wear modest clothes, with their hair tied back, in plaits or in a bun; they were discouraged from dyeing their hair or wearing make-up.

How effective were Nazi policies towards women?

Nazi policies towards women had only mixed success.

Some German women were persuaded by Nazi views and were content to accept Nazi policies towards women. Nazi policies towards women did have the effect the Nazis desired, to an extent. For example, fewer women went to university, the birth rate increased and unemployment amongst German men fell.

However, many women did not support Nazi ideas about womanhood – and some women believed that Nazi ideas harmed the family and degraded women. Some women did not like the Reich Women's Leader, Gertrud Scholtz-Klink, and others felt that the domestic status of women was demeaning (see Sources H, I and J).

Source H

Traudl Junge was a young woman in Nazi Germany. Here she is remembering her youth in Nazi Germany.

Gertrud Scholtz-Klink was the type (of woman) we did not like at all. She was so ugly and wasn't fashionable. We didn't bother about joining her organisation. It didn't attract me or my friends. We were interested in dancing and ballet and didn't care much for political ideas.

Source I

Extract from a letter to a Leipzig newspaper in 1934.

A son, even the youngest, laughs in his mother's face. He regards her as his servant and women in general are merely willing tools of his aims.

Source J

A poster showing women as servants of the Nazi state. It was circulated by the Social Democratic Party – until the party was banned in 1933.

The impact of some Nazi policies towards women was either minor or temporary. For example, by the end of the 1930s, German industry was expanding so fast that the Nazis needed women to return to work. Some Nazi policies were reversed. In 1937, women with marriage loans were allowed to work. Because of this, compared with the five million women in work in 1933, there were actually seven million in work by 1939.

Activity ?

Give Nazi policies towards women a mark out of 10 for effectiveness. Discuss your mark – and your reasons – with other people in the class. Then write a justification for your mark.

Exam-style question, Section B

Study Sources F and J on pages 111–112.

How useful are Sources F and J for an enquiry into the attitudes of Germans towards Nazi policies towards women?

Explain your answer, using Sources F and J and your knowledge of the historical context. **8 marks**

Exam tip

A good answer will consider:

- how useful the information in each source is for this particular enquiry
- how the provenance (i.e. the type of source, its origin, author or purpose) of each source affects how useful it is
- how knowledge of history at that time affects a judgement of how useful each source is.

Summary

- The Nazis believed that women should adopt a modest, traditional appearance, leave professional jobs to men and make marriage and motherhood their duty to the state.
- The Nazis used propaganda and policies to try to put their beliefs into practice.
- The Nazis had several policies to encourage marriage and childbirth. These included the Law for the Encouragement of Marriage, changes to divorce law, the Mother's Cross and Lebensborn.
- The Nazis had several policies to reduce numbers of women in the workforce. These included banning women from some jobs and discouraging women from going to university.
- Nazi policies towards women convinced some Germans and had some impact, but were only effective to a limited or temporary degree.

Checkpoint

Strengthen

S1 What were Nazi ideas towards women regarding marriage, motherhood and childbirth?

S2 What were Nazi ideas about women regarding work and appearance?

S3 What were Nazi policies towards women regarding marriage, motherhood and childbirth?

S4 What were Nazi policies towards women regarding work?

Challenge

C1 Evaluate how much support there was in Germany for Nazi policies towards women.

C2 Evaluate how effective you think Nazi policies towards women were.

How confident do you feel about your answers to these questions? If you are unsure, look again at page 109 for S1–S2, pages 110–111 for S3–S4; for C1–C2, look again at page 112. If you are still unsure about a question, you could join together with others and discuss a joint answer. Your teacher can give you hints.

The aims of Nazi policies concerning the young

The Nazis believed that all parts of society should benefit the German state. We have already seen, for example, how Nazi policies towards the Arts, sport, churches and women were intended to strengthen Germany and the Nazi Party.

Nazi policies for the young had the same aim. Hitler wanted to create what he called the 'Thousand Year Reich' – a Nazi state that would last a very long time. Nazi policies towards the young were not meant to be what was best for young people; they were aimed to strengthen Germany and strengthen the Nazi Party now and in the future.

There are two further things to note about the aims of Nazi policies towards the young.

1. The Nazis believed that boys and girls were equal, but different. They had different strengths to offer Germany. Policies for boys were different from the policies for girls.

2. Hitler knew that many German adults were not Nazi supporters, but he reasoned that if young Germans supported the Nazi Party, this would secure the future of his 'Thousand Year Reich'. So, Nazi propaganda often encouraged young people to see Hitler as a father-figure. Source A shows an example of this.

Source A

This was one of a series of photograph cards for young Germans to collect, published in 1935. These cards could be pasted into a Nazi Party album, called *Adolf Hitler – Pictures of the Life of the Führer*.

What the Nazis believed was best for Germany

- All young Germans should be brought up to be proud Germans who supported a strong, independent Germany.
- All young Germans should be brought up to be supporters of the Nazi Party who believed in Nazi policies.
- All girls should be brought up to be strong and healthy, so that they would be strong wives and healthy, fertile mothers.
- All boys should be brought up to be strong and healthy, to do productive work for the German economy and fight in the German armed forces.

Figure 4.2 The aims of Nazi policies towards the young.

The Nazi youth movement

Before Hitler became Chancellor in January 1933, there were many German youth groups for both boys and girls. Some were youth sections of political parties, such as the Social Democrats, and some were church groups.

The Nazi Party had also set up youth sections for boys and for girls in the 1920s (see page 56). However, these were small in comparison with all the other groups. The table below shows the scale of Nazi youth groups in 1932.

	German youth group membership, 1932
Protestant church youth groups	600,000 boys and girls
Nazi Party youth groups	100,000 boys and girls

In 1933, however, Hitler banned almost all youth groups apart from Nazi groups. From the mid 1930s, more and more pressure was put on young people to join Nazi youth groups. For example, from 1936, all sports facilities for young people were taken over by the Hitler Youth. If young people wanted to use the facilities to play sport, they had to join the Hitler Youth.

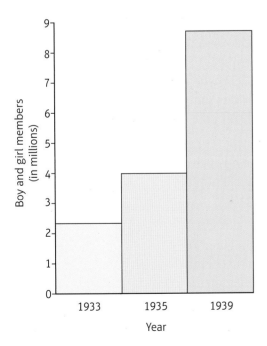

Figure 4.3 Number of 10 to 18-year-olds in Nazi Party youth groups, 1933–39.

In March 1939, it was made compulsory for all young Germans to join Nazi youth groups from the age of 10. Only 'unwanted' minority groups, like Jews, were omitted.

Nazi youth groups for boys

Nazi youth groups were strictly segregated, with separate groups for boys and girls. For boys:

- six to 10-year-olds were in the *Pimpfe* (Little Fellows)
- 10 to 14-year-olds were in the *Deutsche Jungvolk* (German Young People)
- 14 to 18-year-olds were in the *Hitler Jugend* (Hitler Youth).

The Hitler Youth

Political training

Primarily, the Hitler Youth was a political group.

- Members had to swear an oath of loyalty to the Führer.
- They had to attend residential courses where they were told about Nazi ideas.
- The Hitler Youth Leader, Baldur von Schirach, set out a schedule of lessons for every year group of the Hitler Youth to learn. Lessons titles included 'German Heroes', 'Adolf Hitler and his fellow-fighters' and 'The evil of the Jews'.
- Hitler Youth members had to report anyone, even teachers and parents, who was disloyal to the Nazis.

In this way, Hitler hoped to build up a constant supply of citizens who were Nazi Party supporters.

Physical training

The Hitler Youth was also used by the Nazis to make young Germans as fit and healthy as possible.

- There were regular camping and hiking expeditions.
- The Hitler Youth also ran regional and national sports competitions.

Military training

The Hitler Youth was organised to train young German boys to become useful to the state, either as workers or in the armed forces. Therefore, military training was essential.

- Members practised skills useful to troops, such as map-reading and signalling.
- By 1938, 1.2 million boys in the Hitler Youth were being trained in small-arms shooting.
- There were separate military divisions of the Hitler Youth for specialist training, including naval training. The table below show the specialist military sections of the Hitler Youth in 1938.

	Number of boys
Naval Hitler Youth	45,000
Motor Hitler Youth	60,000
Gliding Hitler Youth	55,000
Flying Hitler Youth	74,000

Source B

A photograph of rifle shooting practice for the Hitler Youth, taken in the 1930s.

Character training

The Hitler Youth was also designed to mould young people's characters. Activities stressed the need for comradeship and loyalty, but also competition and ruthlessness (see Source C). For example, boys entering the Jungvolk, aged 10, would swear an oath, saying 'I devote all my energies and strength to the Saviour of our Country, Adolf Hitler. I am willing and ready to give up my life for him, so help me God.'

Hitler Youth members might be drilled by SA instructors, plunged into ice-cold water to toughen them up, forced to undergo lengthy exercises in wintry weather or subjected to harsh punishments for errors or disobeying orders. All this was to build young Germans who obeyed orders even in hardship.

Source C

An extract from a speech by Adolf Hitler in 1933.

My programme for youth is hard. Weakness must be hammered away... I want a brutal, domineering, fearless, cruel youth. It must bear pain. There must be nothing weak and gentle about it... That is how I will create the New Order.

Extend your knowledge

Attending meetings

In September 1934, when the number of people attending the Hitler Youth meetings in Hamburg fell, its leaders sent this note to the members and their parents.

'You are not turning up to do your duty. Instead you are pursuing private pleasures. The 'I' counts more amongst you than the Nazi 'we'. You are sinning against the nation.'

This note gives an important insight into the aims of the Hitler Youth. Membership was not compulsory at this time. Why then do you think that Hitler Youth leaders thought it was such a bad thing that young people were failing to attend?

The League of German Maidens

The Nazi Party created separate youth groups for girls.

- 10 to 14-year-olds belonged to the *Jungmädel* (Young Maidens).
- 14 to 21-year-olds were in the *Bund Deutscher Mädel*, or BDM (League of German Maidens).

Some of the activities of the BDM were the same for girls as the activities for boys in the Hitler Youth.

- There were political activities, just like for boys, including rallies and oaths of allegiance (see Source D).
- There were also physical and character-building activities, just like for boys. For example, camping and marching were compulsory (see Source E).

However, the girls in the BDM were trained to do different tasks from the boys in the Hitler Youth. For example, they did not receive any military training.

- Girls were trained to cook, iron, make beds, sew and generally to prepare to be a housewife.
- Girls were also taught the importance of 'racial hygiene' – the idea that they should keep the German race 'pure' by only marrying Aryan men. The Nazis believed that the Aryan race was superior to all other races. They were often portrayed with blond hair and blue eyes.

Source D

A photograph of a BDM gathering in 1933. New members, with raised hands, swear allegiance to Hitler in front of the Nazi Youth Leader von Schirach.

Source E

A German woman, Ilse Mckee, remembering her time in the BDM. This was originally published in 1966, in a book of contemporary accounts of life in Nazi Germany between 1933 and 1939.

We had to be present at every public meeting and at youth rallies and sports. The weekends were crammed full with outings, camping, and marches when we carried heavy packs on our backs. It was all fun in a way, and we certainly got plenty of exercise, but it had a bad effect on our school reports. There was hardly ever any time for homework.

... girls of my age had to attend evening classes twice weekly. The evening classes were conducted by young girls, usually hardly older than we were ourselves... we were of course lectured on a lot of Nazi ideology, and most of this went over our heads... we were told from a very early age to prepare for motherhood, as the mother in the eyes of our beloved leader... was the most important person in the nation. We were Germany's hope and Germany's future.

Did Nazi youth groups achieve Nazi aims?

Some young people were enthusiastic and committed Hitler Youth members. However, some were less keen. They did not enjoy being forced to do activities they did not enjoy or believe in. Many German adults had reservations, too. For example, many parents believed they were being undermined by Nazi youth groups, as the groups taught that loyalty should ultimately lie with the Nazi state, and not with your family.

Sources F and G give differing views on the Hitler Youth – both are accounts written many years after the events took place.

Source F

A. Klonne, describing his memories of the Hitler Youth in his book, *Youth in the Third Reich*, published in 1982.

What I liked about the Hitler Youth was the comradeship. I was full of enthusiasm. What boy isn't fired by ideals such as comradeship, loyalty and honour and the trips off into the countryside and sport? Later... negative aspects became obvious. The compulsion and obedience were unpleasant. I preferred people to have a will of their own... In our troop, the activity was almost entirely boring military drill.

Source G

Henrik Metelmann was a member of the Hitler Youth in the 1930s. He wrote a book in 1980 explaining his experiences in Nazi Germany.

You felt you belonged to a great nation again. I was helping to build a strong Germany. But my father felt differently. He warned, "Henrik, don't tell them what I am saying to you." I argued with my father, because I was a great believer in the Hitler regime, which was against his background as a working man.

Activities ?

1 List the Nazis' aims for German youth.

2 Make a table with two columns, showing the ways that Nazi youth groups were the same or different for boys and girls.

3 Hold a class discussion. Were Nazi youth groups mainly for a) political indoctrination, b) military training or c) character building? Then write your opinion, with reasons.

Interpretation 1

An extract from *Modern Germany*, by V. R. Berghahn (1982).

(The Hitler Youth's)… romantic appeal to a spirit of friendship and community, to sacrifice and the ideal of a well-ordered society, together with charismatic leadership, met strong emotional needs among young people. There was also an element of rebellion against parents and teachers. So they went off, in Boy Scout fashion, to weekend camps and hikes, listening to the persuasive speeches of their leaders. It is not surprising that so many teenagers fell under the spell of the slogans by the fireside.

Exam-style question, Section B

Study Source F.

Give **two** things you can infer from Source F about the Hitler Youth. **4 marks**

Exam tip

This question tests source analysis, specifically the skill of making inferences.

A good answer will work out what can be inferred about the Hitler Youth using selected details in the source.

Nazi control of the young through education

In 1933, all children in Germany went to school until the age of 14; after that, attendance at school was voluntary. Boys and girls went to separate schools. Most schools were controlled by local councils, though some were run by the Church.

All this changed after Hitler came to power. He wanted the young to be the long-term security of his Third Reich (see Source H). Hitler believed that even if some adults did not believe in Nazi ideas, if children were taught from a young age to believe, they would follow Hitler, no matter what.

In 1934, a leading Nazi, Bernhard Rust, was made Education Minister. Rust saw schools as a way of controlling the views of young Germans and once said that 'the whole purpose of education is to create Nazis'. During the 1930s, he made a series of changes to bring all schools under the control of the Nazis.

Source H

An extract from Hitler's speech on May Day 1933.

When an opponent declares "I will not support you," I calmly say, "Your child belongs to us already. How important are you? You will soon be gone. Your children however now stand in our camp."

Nazi control of teachers

One way that the Nazis controlled the education of young Germans was by controlling teachers.

- As early as April 1933, the Nazis passed a law giving them the power to sack teachers and headteachers they didn't approve of. In just one German state, Prussia, Rust sacked over 180 secondary headteachers.
- All teachers had to swear an oath of loyalty to Hitler and had to join the Nazi Teachers' League.
- The Nazi Teachers' League ran political education courses for teachers, setting out the Nazi ideas which teachers should support. By 1939, over 200,000 teachers had attended the courses.

Having taken control of teachers, the Nazis then expected teachers to behave as Nazis.

- Teachers taught students to do the Nazi salute.
- They started and ended each lesson with the children saying 'Heil Hitler'.
- Nazi posters and flags decorated classrooms.

Nazi control of the curriculum

The curriculum is what is taught in schools. Another way the Nazis controlled young Germans was to take control of the curriculum.

- New school subjects were added, such as Race Studies. In this subject, German children were taught how to classify racial groups and were told that Aryans were superior and that they should not marry inferior races such as Jews.
- Traditional subjects, such as mathematics, were changed to make them more useful to the kind of society Nazis wanted, or to make them vehicles for Nazi ideas.
- The amount of time in schools for PE and sport was doubled. By 1939, they took up about one-sixth of lesson time. This was to create strong workers, soldiers and healthy mothers.
- The curriculum was different for boys and girls. For example, domestic science, including cookery and needlework, became compulsory for girls in order to make them better wives and mothers.
- From 1935, all new textbooks had to be approved by the Nazis. New history books, for example, explained that the Treaty of Versailles was a 'stab in the back' for Germany, planned by the Socialists, and that Jews were evil. *Mein Kampf* was made a compulsory school text.
- Pupils gathered together in school halls to listen to major political speeches on the radio.

Source J

A mathematics question from a German textbook approved by the Nazis.

A plane takes off carrying 12 bombs, each weighing 10 kilos. It bombs Warsaw, the world centre of Jews. At take-off, it had 1,500 kilos of fuel and weighed 8 tonnes. When it returned from its crusade, it had 230 kilos of fuel left. What was the weight of the aircraft?

Extend your knowledge

New types of schools

In 1933, Bernhard Rust set up three **Napolas**. These were boarding schools which were intended to train the future leaders of Germany. By 1939, there were 16 Napolas.

- Pupils were selected for these schools by being tested in examinations and sports and then examined by doctors. Only the most intelligent, competitive, aggressive and racially pure children were selected.
- Pupils were not taught by teachers, but by selected members of the SA and the SS.
- The curriculum was similar to other schools, but with no religious education and more sport.
- At the end of their schooling, the pupils went into the army or the SS or the police as officers.

Source I

A photograph taken in 1934 showing German students giving the Nazi salute.

THINKING HISTORICALLY Evidence (4a&b)

The 'weight' of evidence

One useful idea to have in mind when interpreting historical sources is 'consistency' (whether or not sources support each other).

If a number of sources appear to suggest the same conclusion about the past, then it can be tempting to feel more confident about accepting this conclusion.

However, we should not assume that just because an idea is in many sources, it must be correct. We should also consider the *nature* of the sources and the *reasons why* sources might seem to disagree.

Sources K and L could be used by the historian to build up a picture of how much political interference there was in schools under the Nazis.

1 Explain how Sources K and L differ in their views of Nazi political interference in schools.

2 How can the different views in these sources about political interference in schools be explained? Why do they say different things? Write down as many reasons as you can.

Discuss the following in groups:

3 Suppose the historian had ten more sources that agreed broadly with Source K and only four that agreed with Source L. Would this mean that Source K was nearer to the truth? Explain your answer.

4 What else should we consider, apart from the 'the balance of the evidence', when drawing conclusions from sources such as these?

Source K

Extracts from *The Law for the Restoration of the Professional Civil Service*, 7 April 1933

The Reich Government has enacted the following Law: ... civil servants [including teachers] may be dismissed from office in accordance with the following regulations.

Civil servants [including teachers] who have entered the service since November 9, 1918, without possessing the required or customary educational background or other qualifications are to be dismissed from the service.

Civil servants [including teachers] who are not of Aryan descent are to be retired.

Civil servants [including teachers] whose previous political activities suggest that they will not, at all times, give their fullest support to the national State, can be dismissed from the service.

Reich Chancellor Adolf Hitler

Source L

A school pupil comments on life in the mid 1930s.

No one in our class ever read *Mein Kampf*. I myself had only used the book for quotations.

In general we didn't know much about National Socialist ideas. Even anti-Semitism was taught rather a little at school, for instance through Richard Wagner's essay 'The Jews in Music'. Outside school the display copies of *Der Stürmer* [a Nazi newspaper] made the idea seem ridiculous, if anything.

Nevertheless, we were politically programmed: programmed to obey orders, to cultivate the soldierly 'virtue' of standing to attention and saying 'Yes, Sir', and to switch our minds off when the magic word 'fatherland' was uttered and Germany's honour and greatness were invoked.

Activities

1   To establish the purpose of Nazi policies towards schools, make a table with the following headings.

Teaching Nazi beliefs	Making Germany stronger	Treating boys and girls differently	Meeting the needs of individual children

  a   Using the information on pages 120–121, write as much as you can about schools in Nazi Germany under each heading.

  b   When you have finished, write a paragraph to say what your table suggests were the main aims of schools in Nazi Germany.

  c   How does your conclusion fit with the ideas of Adolf Hitler and Bernhard Rust?

Summary

- The Nazis believed that young Germans should be brought up to be useful Germans and supporters of Nazi ideas.
- They believed that boys and girls should be brought up to be different.
- Nazi youth groups, such as the Hitler Youth and the League of German Maidens, were organised to create strong, healthy Germans and supporters of Nazi ideas.
- Schools in Nazi Germany were organised to create useful German adults and Nazi supporters.
- The Nazis shaped the development of young Germans by controlling teachers and the curriculum.

Checkpoint

Strengthen

S1 Describe Nazi aims towards the young.

S2 How were Nazi youth groups organised?

S3 How were Nazi schools organised?

Challenge

C1 Explain how the features of Nazi youth groups were intended to achieve Nazi aims towards the young.

C2 Explain how the features of Nazi schools were intended to achieve Nazi aims towards the young.

How confident do you feel about your answers to these questions? If you are unsure, look again at page 114 for S1, pages 115–118 for S2, pages 119–120 for S3. If you are still unsure about a question, you could join together with others and discuss a joint answer. Your teacher can give you hints.

Nazi policies to reduce unemployment

In January 1933, when Hitler became Chancellor, about five million Germans were unemployed – about 25% of the labour force. So, reducing unemployment was a priority for Hitler. There were two reasons for this.

1 Unemployment was politically dangerous to Hitler. Unemployed workers suffered poor living conditions and demanded help. If Hitler could not help them, they may begin to support the Communist Party, Hitler's rivals.

2 The Nazis believed that unemployed workers were a waste of resources and a burden on society. To remove this burden, they wanted as many people as possible in useful work, in the service of the country.

By 1939, unemployment had fallen to about half a million people (see Figure 4.4). How did the Nazis achieve this?

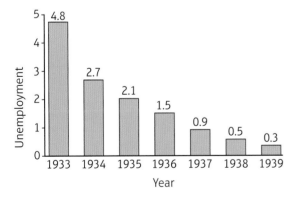

Figure 4.4 Unemployment (in millions) in Germany, 1933–39.

Labour Service (RAD)

In 1933, the Nazis set up the *Reichs Arbeits Dienst,* or RAD – the National Labour Service. This provided paid work for the unemployed.

The RAD provided workers for public works, such as repairing roads, planting trees and draining marshes. Apart from giving men work, these projects were also good for Germany as a whole.

At first, the RAD was voluntary. However, from 1935, it was made compulsory for all young men to serve for six months in the RAD. The number of people in the RAD reached 422,000 in 1935.

However, the RAD was not popular. It was organised like an army – workers wore uniforms, lived in camps and did military drill and parades as well as work. Rates of pay were very low and some complained of poor food and working conditions. Some men saw the RAD as service for the Nazi Party or military service rather than normal employment.

Source A

A photograph of Hitler greeting men in the Labour Service (RAD) at a Nazi Party rally in Nuremberg in 1938.

Autobahns

Another scheme which the Nazis used to reduce unemployment was the *autobahn* (motorway) project. The Nazis planned a 7,000 mile network of dual-carriageway roads to improve transport around Germany.

- In September 1933, Hitler personally started construction of the very first autobahn (see Source B) and the first stretch of motorway was opened in May 1935.
- By 1935, 125,000 men were employed building motorways and by 1938, 3,500 km had been finished.

The *autobahn* project was just one example of a huge number of public works schemes financed by the Nazis. They created public buildings, bridges, coastal walls and sports facilities. Spending on public works grew from 18 billion marks in 1933 to 38 billion marks in 1938.

Public works such as these created many jobs in the construction industry. Better roads and bridges also meant quicker and cheaper transport for German industry and agriculture. This helped to boost the sale of German goods at home and abroad, creating even more jobs in the rest of the German economy.

Source B

A photograph taken in 1933. It shows Hitler personally 'turning the first turf' to start construction of the first autobahn.

Rearmament

One of Hitler's main aims in government was boosting Germany's armed forces (see Source C).

Rearmament helped to reduce unemployment in two ways.

1 The Treaty of Versailles had limited the size of Germany's armed forces. Hitler defied these limits. In 1935, he announced military conscription. All young German men would have to serve a period in the German armed forces. By 1939, there were 1,360,000 men in the German armed forces (see Figure 4.5). This helped to reduce the number of unemployed.

2 Hitler's bigger armed forces needed more arms and equipment. Government spending on arms in 1933 was 3.5 billion marks. By 1939, this had grown to 26 billion marks. This caused a big jump in employment in the arms industry. For example, in 1933, there were only 4,000 people employed in the aircraft construction industry. By 1935, this had grown to 72,000.

Source C

From a speech by Hitler to his ministers in February 1933.

The next five years in Germany must be devoted to the rearmament of Germany. Every job creation scheme must be judged by whether it helps rearmament... Germany's position in the world will depend on the position of Germany's armed forces. Upon this, the position of Germany's economy also depends.

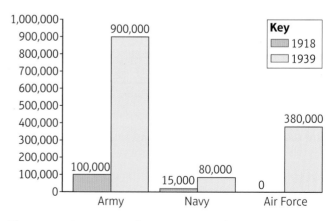

Figure 4.5 Expansion of German armed forces, 1918–39.

Invisible unemployment

Some historians say that the Nazis didn't really reduce unemployment. For example, some historians say that the real number of unemployed people was higher than the official figures by almost one and half million people. The Nazis just found ways to reduce the number of people **recorded** as unemployed. In other words, they made some unemployment 'invisible'. They did this in several ways.

- Women and Jews who may have wanted jobs were forced to give up work; these are sometimes called the invisible unemployed.
- Men who would have been unemployed were found jobs in the Labour Service or public works.
- People who could only find part-time work were counted as fully employed.

Figure 4.6 gives more details of the ways that the Nazis 'hid' the real number of unemployed.

The Labour Service
By the middle of the 1930s, there were about half a million 'unemployed' people in the Labour Service. These did not show up in unemployment figures.

Rearmament
By 1939, many jobs depended upon massive armaments orders. In normal peacetime, these jobs would not exist.

Women and Jews
The Nazis forced women and Jews to give up work. These unemployed did not show up on the unemployment figures.

The SA, SS and Gestapo
The Nazis used public money to employ hundreds of thousands of men in their own security forces. Some would say that these were not 'real' jobs.

Changing statistics
The Nazis changed the way that unemployment statistics were calculated after 1933. From 1935, for example, people in part-time jobs were counted amongst the full-time employed.

'Reducing' unemployment figures

The armed forces
By 1939, over 1.3 million men were in the armed forces. In normal peacetime, most of these men would need jobs

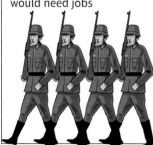

Prisons
The Nazis put hundreds of thousands into prisons or concentration camps. This made unemployment look lower than it would in normal times.

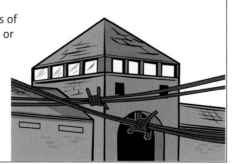

Public works
The Nazis had a huge programme of public works in the 1930s. This was much too expensive to afford for long, so the jobs it created were not 'real' jobs.

Figure 4.6 Ways in which the Nazis 'hid' the real level of unemployment.

Overall verdict on unemployment in Nazi Germany

The achievement of the Nazis in reducing the official unemployment figures in Germany by over four million was remarkable. In Britain, in comparison, unemployment fell by only about one million in the 1930s. Reducing unemployment helped to prevent any build-up of public resentment towards the Nazis. However, it must be remembered that:

* unemployment was falling everywhere in the 1930s as countries recovered from the Great Depression
* some unemployed people, such as Jews, women and political prisoners, were not counted in official figures
* some jobs created by the Nazis (for example, in the armaments industry, in the armed forces, in the Nazi security forces and in the Labour Service) were not 'real' jobs – they were created by the economy
* some jobs in Nazi Germany were supported by very high levels of government spending which could not have been maintained in the long run.

Activities ?

1 Give two reasons why Hitler was so keen to reduce unemployment in Nazi Germany.

2 Write a list of the types of Germans who would have benefitted from Nazi policies towards unemployment and a list of the types of Germans who might have suffered.

3 Hold a class debate on this proposition: *'Hitler's two main aims towards unemployment were a) to get people into jobs and b) to prevent unemployment creating political unrest. He was completely successful in both'*. Afterwards, write your own opinion.

Changes in the standard of living

The standard of living is a measure which tells us whether people's lives are getting better or worse. It is not easy to measure the changes in standard of living because:

* sometimes, the standard of living goes up for some people, but down for others
* sometimes, some aspects of people's lives get better and other aspects get worse
* sometimes people can become wealthier but their enjoyment of life gets worse – or vice versa.

With this in mind, what happened to the standard of living of German people in Nazi Germany?

Employment

More people in work in Germany in 1939 meant more workers enjoying the benefits of a regular income. This could be seen as evidence of a rise in the standard of living. However, not everyone benefited equally. Some people, such as Jews, found it increasingly difficult to get jobs. Also, some workers, like many of those in the Labour Service, did not enjoy their jobs.

Wages

In general, the wages of German workers improved under the Nazis. The improvement was quite slow from 1933 to 1936, but better between 1936 and 1939, when wages rose quite quickly (see table opposite). However, the overall figures hide big variations. The wages of some workers, such as those in the armaments industries, rose more than others, such as those in the Labour Service.

Year	Rise in wages compared with 1933
1934	6%
1936	9%
1939	20%

There is also another complication to consider. The price of goods also rose in the 1930s. According to some historians, food prices in Germany rose by 20% between 1933 and 1939 – so, for some workers, the benefit of high wages was cancelled out by higher prices. This caused variations in the standard of living.

Year	Rise in sale of goods compared with 1933
1934	14%
1936	25%
1939	45%

- High earners, like skilled workers, could pay the extra cost of food and have money left over to buy more luxury goods – so the standard of living of some Germans seems to have gone up quite a lot. The number of car owners in Germany, for example, trebled in the 1930s.
- However, low earners, like unskilled workers, had to use their extra wages to cover the higher costs for essentials, like food.

Hours worked

Another factor which affected the standard of living was the length of the working week. On average, the working week for German workers rose from about 43 hours in 1933 to about 49 hours in 1939. So, even workers whose wages went up had to work longer to earn them.

Nazi organisations which affected the standard of living of workers

The Nazis organised the German economy to benefit the German state, which is why they spent so much government money on schemes like rearmament and public works.

Hitler knew that he must also make sure that the economy benefitted German workers. If German workers were not happy, the Nazis could start losing support. The Nazis therefore had a series of organisations which were meant to improve the lives of German workers. The three main ones were: **The Labour Front (DAF)**, **Strength Through Joy (KdF)** and **The Beauty of Labour (SdA)**.

The Labour Front (DAF)

Normally, trade unions help to protect and improve the standard of living of workers. However, Hitler believed that trade unions supported his political rivals, the Communist Party. He also believed that powerful trade unions could disrupt the economy, for example, by calling strikes. So, in 1933, the Nazi government banned trade unions. This was not a good start for the standard of living of German workers.

In place of trade unions, Hitler set up the DAF (*Deutsche Arbeitsfront*, or German Labour Front) in 1933. The DAF protected the rights of workers. For example, the DAF set out:

- the rights of workers in the workplace
- maximum length of the working week
- minimum pay levels.

The DAF regulated what employers could do and, in this sense, it protected the standard of living of German workers. However, in some ways German workers were worse off under the DAF than they had been under trade unions.

- Workers had lost their right to negotiate improvements in pay and conditions with their employers.
- The maximum length of the working week set by the DAF went up by about six hours per week.
- The DAF had the power to punish workers who disrupted production.

Overall, the role of the DAF was to control both employers and employees. This was to ensure that businesses worked – not for the best interests of business owners or workers, but the best interests of the state.

Strength through Joy (KdF)

Hitler realised that the loss of trade unions could be a source of unrest amongst German workers. Because of this, the Nazis set up another organisation in 1933 to improve the standard of living of workers. It was named Strength through Joy (*Kraft durch Freude*, or KdF). It was a division of the DAF.

The purpose of the KdF was to make the benefits of work more enjoyable, so that Germans would see their work as a way to a happy life, as well as making the nation stronger.

One way the KdF improved the benefits of work was to provide leisure activities for workers. These included sports events, films, theatre shows, outings and even foreign travel. Most activities were low key, but they were well supported (see Source D). The most loyal workers could even win impressive holidays. Most workers were expected to join the KdF and were encouraged to take part in its activities. By 1936, there were 35 million members of the KdF.

Source D

Official Nazi figures for a selection of Strength through Joy activities in the Berlin area, 1933–39.

Type of event	No. of events	No. of people involved
Lectures	19,000	1,000,000
Theatre performances	21,000	11,000,000
Museum tours	60,000	2,500,000
Sports events	400	1,500,000
Hikes	6,000	125,000
Holidays and cruises	1,000	700,000

Volkswagen – the 'people's car'

This was another scheme for workers run by the KdF. Hitler asked Ferdinand Porsche to design a car for four people which would travel 40 miles to the gallon and which the average German could afford. Porsche designed the Volkswagen. The KdF encouraged workers to give five marks per week from their wages, which would eventually entitle them to a new Volkswagen. The money set up factories to make the cars. But from 1938, the factories switched to production of armaments. No workers ever saw their money or their Volkswagen.

Source E

A KdF poster, from 1939. It urged workers to give 'just 5 marks a week to drive your own car'.

Beauty of Labour (SdA)

One division of the KdF which affected the standard of living of German workers was the Beauty of Labour – *Schönheit der Arbeit* – or SdA. This campaigned to get employers to provide better facilities for workers, like better toilets, changing rooms, showers and canteens. The SdA gave employers tax breaks to help with building and decorating costs. By 1938, the Nazi Party claimed that nearly 34,000 companies had improved their facilities.

However, it was normal for employers to expect workers to do the building and decorating themselves, after work hours and at no extra pay. Some employers even threatened those who did not volunteer with dismissal.

However, it was normal for employers to expect workers to do the building and decorating themselves, after work and at no extra pay. Some employers even threatened those who did not volunteer with dismissal.

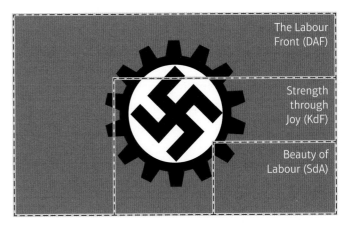

Figure 4.7 The Beauty of Labour was a division of Strength through Joy. Strength through Joy was a division of the Labour Front. Beauty of Labour was a division of Strength through Joy.

Overall judgement on the standard of living in Nazi Germany

As so many aspects of workers' lives were changing in Nazi Germany, it is difficult to make an overall judgement about whether living standards improved or not. For example, the standard of living may have improved for some people and not others, depending on their circumstances. Interpretation 1 and 2 discuss the real and alleged benefits for German people under the Nazis.

Interpretation 1

From *Life in Germany*, by Steve Waugh published in 2009.

From 1936 to 1939 wages increased, but this was due to a longer working day rather than an increase in hourly wage rates. In addition, the cost of living rose in the 1930's, which meant that real wages (how much workers could buy) actually fell. There were also food shortages, because the government reduced agricultural production to keep up prices [to help farmers].

129

Interpretation 2

From *Nationalism, dictatorship and democracy in 20th Century Europe*, by Hall, Shuter, Brown and Williams, published in 2015.

For Germans who conformed to Nazi expectations, living standards went up. Unemployment dropped. Nazi statistics show that real wages rose... though only if a worker worked overtime. The 'Strength Through Joy' programme provided many extras. Some (benefits), such as loans [and] medical care... were real enough.

Exam-style question, Section B

Suggest **one** reason why Interpretations 1 and 2 (pages 129 and 130) give different views about the standard of living of German workers in Nazi Germany.

You may use Sources A and D (pages 123 and 128) to help explain your answer. **4 marks**

Exam tip

A good answer will analyse both interpretations and explain a possible reason why they give different impressions of the quality of life of German workers under the Nazis.

You should try to strengthen your explanation by referring to the sources or information of your own about the quality of life of German workers.

Interpretations vary for many reasons, for example because they are based on different sources, give partial pictures of the situation or stress different aspects of a situation.

Summary

- Reducing unemployment was a priority for Hitler, for political and economic reasons.
- The Nazis used a variety of methods to reduce unemployment. These included the National Labour Service, the autobahn project and rearmament.
- As well as official unemployment levels, Nazi Germany also had 'invisible unemployment'.
- There were many changes to the standard of living of workers in Nazi Germany. These included changes to unemployment, wages, prices, and consumption of luxuries.
- The Labour Front, including Strength through Joy and the Beauty of Labour, also affected the standard of living of German workers.

Checkpoint

Strengthen

S1 What happened to unemployment in Nazi Germany?

S2 In what ways did the Nazis try to reduce unemployment?

S3 Describe changes in wages, prices and sale of luxury goods in Nazi Germany.

S4 What was the impact on the standard of living of German workers of the Labour Front, Strength through Joy and the Beauty of Labour?

Challenge

C1 Give a reasoned opinion about how much unemployment fell in Nazi Germany.

C2 Give a reasoned opinion about whether the standard of living of workers rose or fell in Nazi Germany.

How confident do you feel about your answers to these questions? If you are unsure, look again at pages 124–126 for S1–S2 and pages 127–129 for S3–S4. For C1–C2, discuss with other people in class. Your teacher can provide hints.

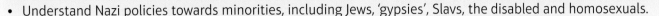
Nazi racial beliefs and policies

Nazi policies were intended to make the German state as strong as possible. Policies for German children, women, workers, justice, churches and art were all shaped to strengthen the German state.

The Nazis also believed that, to make the German state strong, the German **population** needed to be strong. This belief affected their policy towards minorities in the population. It was a belief with two strands: **eugenics** and **racial hygiene**.

Eugenics

Eugenics is the science of selective breeding. It became popular in Europe from the 1880s. Scientists took the ideas of Charles Darwin – who explained that species changed over time through evolution – and explored how these changes could be controlled to produce 'better' human beings. An example of this would be by selecting the 'best' parents, or by preventing reproduction by 'unsuitable' parents, to create the best child possible.

The Nazis took these ideas and applied them to their policies. Eugenics became a subject in schools. They also encouraged reproduction by the 'best' Germans and prevented those they considered 'unsuitable'. This was achieved by sterilising them – a medical procedure that meant they could not have children.

Racial hygiene

Eugenics is about selecting the 'best' parents, from any race. The Nazis took this a stage further. They wanted to choose the best parents from just one race- the Aryan race. They believed that the Aryan race was superior to all others. The Aryan race described by the Nazis came from a specific part of Europe, and the Nazis believed they were superior to all other races. Because of this, they adopted policies to make Germany as Aryan as possible.

In schools, in the Hitler Youth and in propaganda, the Nazis taught racial hygiene – the idea that Aryan Germans should only reproduce with other Aryans, to make their offspring 'pure' Aryan, unspoiled by other racial characteristics. They also applied this belief to their policies and passed laws to prevent mixed-race marriages.

Source A

A photograph of eugenics being taught iin the early 1940s. The chart on the left shows the 'inheritance of musical talent.' The chart on right shows that certain diseases, like hemophilia, can be inherited.

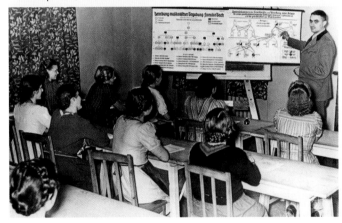

Hitler's views

In 1925, Hitler set out his racial views in *Mein Kampf*. He claimed that there was a hierarchy of races. He believed:

- the Aryan race was the superior race – the *Herrenvolk* or master race – portrayed as tall, blond, blue-eyed and athletic.
- other races, such as the Slavs of Eastern Europe, were *Untermenschen* – sub-humans
- the worst of the *Untermenschen* were 'gypsies' and Jews. Later, Hitler deemed them *Lebensunwertes* – which means unworthy of life.

These beliefs also affected Nazi policies – for example, by shaping who the Nazis allowed to be German citizens.

Anti-Semitism

Nazi ideas about eugenics and racial hygiene were particularly aimed against the Jews. Anti-Jewish views, sometimes called anti-Semitism, had been common throughout Europe for many centuries, for many reasons.

- Their religion, customs and looks made Jews stand out as 'different'.
- Some Christians hated Jews, as they blamed them for the execution of Christ.
- Some Jews were very successful in finance and business, creating jealousy towards them.

By the 1930s, anti-Semitism had become particularly strong in Germany. There were several reasons.

- Germany was only united as a single country in 1871. Efforts by German nationalists to unite the country included some positive forces, such as the promotion of German heroes in mythology, music and science. It also led, however, to a heightened opposition to Germany's 'enemies' including the British Empire, Communism and minority groups, such as the Jews.
- When times are hard, people often look for people to blame. The German defeat in the First World War, the Treaty of Versailles, inflation in 1923 and the German economic depression of 1929–33 were all blamed on the Jews – with very little evidence – by German nationalist politicians.
- Hitler was one of many nationalist politicians in Germany who hated the Jews (see Source D on page 134). His own bitterness towards Jews was given complete freedom when he came to power in 1933.

- Germans with more moderate views allowed themselves to be influenced by Nazi propaganda (see Source B) and turned a blind eye to – or even participated in – Nazi persecution of the Jews.

Source B

A Nazi poster, from 1937. The writing says 'the eternal Jew'. The poster was used to turn people against Jews.

Activities

1 **The 15 Second Challenge!** In pairs, try to speak for 15 seconds – without hesitation, deviation or repetition – on each of the following: a) eugenics, b) racial hygiene, c) Hitler's ideas on race, d) anti-Semitism. Afterwards, write a short paragraph on each to record what you know about them.

2 Source B shows Jews as different from 'normal' Germans – ugly, sinister, cruel, money-grabbing supporters of communism. Can you find the aspects of the poster that suggest these characteristics?

3 Nazi racial beliefs led to the persecution of minorities during the 1930s. To help you record the events of this persecution, make a horizontal timeline showing the years 1933 to 1939.

   a Above the line, record the events showing the persecution of minority groups on pages 133–134.

   b Below the line, record the events showing the persecution of the Jews on pages 134–137.

The treatment of minorities

Slavs

The Slavs were ancient tribes of people who migrated into Europe from the east. Their modern descendants are found in large areas across Eastern Europe. By the 1930s, many people of Slavic origin lived in Germany.

- Nazi propaganda and school lessons constantly told Germans that the Slavs were *Untermenschen* – sub-humans. The Nazis insisted that, like Jews and 'gypsies', they were of a different origin from Aryan Germans and needed to be treated differently.
- The Nazis threatened to invade Slav countries in Eastern Europe for *Lebensraum* – extra living space – for Germany's people.
- However, before the Second World War, Slavs were persecuted less than some other minorities.

'Gypsies'

'Gypsies' was the name used by the Nazis for the Roma people. They typically lived an itinerant lifestyle, travelling from place to place. There were about 26,000 'gypsies' in Germany in the early 1930s. The Nazis believed they did not work enough or contribute enough taxes. They believed that 'gypsies' posed a threat to the racial purity of Germany.

- After 1933, 'gypsies' were often arrested as social nuisances and sent to concentration camps.
- From 1936, some were forced to live in special camps. One camp in Berlin contained 600 'gypsies', who had been forcibly rounded up. It had just two latrines, three water taps and no electricity.
- In 1938, 'gypsies' were banned from travelling in groups. They were rounded up, put on a register of 'gypsies' and tested for racial characteristics. If they 'failed' the test, they lost German citizenship and social benefits.
- In 1939, orders were given to prepare all 'gypsies' for deportation. This meant that they would be forcibly removed from Germany.

Homosexuals

The Nazis believed that homosexuals lowered moral standards and spoiled the purity of the German race.

- In 1935, the Nazis strengthened the laws against homosexuality. As a result, in 1934, 766 males were imprisoned for homosexuality. In 1936, this number was over 4,000. In 1938, it was 8,000.
- Released homosexual prisoners were often sent to concentration camps: 5,000 German homosexuals died there.
- Nazi laws also encouraged the voluntary castration of homosexuals.

People with disabilities

The Nazis believed that people with disabilities were a burden on society and weakened racial purity (see Source C).

- In 1933, the Nazis passed the **Law for the Prevention of Hereditarily Diseased Offspring**. This made it compulsory for people to be sterilised if they were mentally ill, alcoholic, deformed, epileptic, deaf or blind. 400,000 people were sterilised, using surgical operations, by 1939.
- In 1939, the Nazis ordered that babies with severe mental or physical disabilities should be killed by starvation or lethal overdose of drugs. This became known as the **T4 Programme**. Eventually, juveniles up to 17 years old with disabilities were included and over 5,000 children with disabilities were killed.

Source C

A Nazi poster from 1938. It says '60,000 Reichmarks. This is what the person suffering from hereditary defects costs the Community of Germans during his lifetime. Fellow Citizen, that is your money too.'

The persecution of the Jews

There were only 437,000 Jews in Germany in 1933 – less than 1% of the population. But before Hitler became Chancellor in 1933, he had made clear that action against the Jews would be a priority.

Source D

Hitler, speaking to an acquaintance, Josef Hell, in 1922.

If I am ever in power, the destruction of the Jews will be my first and most important job. I shall have gallows after gallows erected in Munich. Then the Jews will be hanged one after another, and they will stay hanging till they stink... Exactly the same procedure will be followed in other cities until Germany is cleansed of the last Jew.

Persecution begins (1933)

As the Nazis gradually took control of education, the press and the Arts, Nazi propaganda, calling Jews 'vermin' and 'filth' and describing them as evil and scheming, flooded Germany through schools, newspapers and films.

It is difficult to know how this propaganda affected the treatment of Jews by ordinary Germans, but, where the Nazis had influence, they began to discriminate against Jews. Jews were gradually excluded from positions of power or wealth. For example:

- from April 1933, Jews were banned from government jobs and Jewish civil servants and teachers were sacked
- from September 1933, Jews were banned from inheriting land
- from May 1935, Jews were banned from the army.

Nazis who controlled local councils began to follow the lead of the Nazi government.

- From 1934, some local councils banned Jews from parks and swimming pools.
- Others provided separate yellow park benches for Jews, to keep 'normal' Germans 'safe'.

The boycott of Jewish shops and businesses (1933)

One aspect of this early persecution of Jews was a Nazi campaign against Jewish shops and businesses.

On 30 March 1933, the Nazi Party announced that, from 10 a.m. on 1 April, an official boycott would begin of all Jewish businesses, doctors and lawyers. SA stormtroopers were sent to paint Jewish stars or the word *Jude* (Jew) outside Jewish businesses. They then stood outside with banners, discouraging people from going inside.

Source E

A photograph of the boycotting of Jewish shops in 1933. The Nazi sign says *Germans, defend yourselves. Don't buy from Jews.*

The Nuremberg Laws (1935)

As the Nazis established themselves in power, persecution became worse. On 15 September 1935, a set of changes called the Nuremberg Laws were passed. Two of these laws increased the persecution of the Jews.

The Reich Law on Citizenship

- This law stated that only those of German blood could be German citizens.
- Jews became German 'subjects', not citizens.
- They lost the rights of citizenship, the right to vote and the right to hold government office or German passports.

The Reich Law for the Protection of German Blood and Honour

- This law forbade Jews from marrying German citizens.
- It also forbade sexual relations between Jews and German citizens.

Source F

A photograph from 1933 of a Jewish man, on the right, being accused of having a German girlfriend. They have both been forced by SA and SS members to walk the streets with signs admitting their 'crime'.

Extend your knowledge

The Reich Law on Citizenship of 1935

The Reich Law on Citizenship of 1935 banned Jews from being German citizens. To do this, it had to define what a Jew was. The definition which the law adopted was that anyone with three or four grandparents who practised the Jewish religion would be considered to be a Jew.

This was a fairly random definition. It included 50,000 Jews who had become Christians. It excluded 200,000 practising Jews who had only one or two Jewish grandparents.

From 1938, matters became more ominous for Jews.

- From March 1938, Jews had to register all of their possessions – making it easier for the government to confiscate them.
- From July 1938, Jews had to carry identity cards, making it easier for them to be persecuted.

And then, in November 1938, persecution of the Jews became even worse.

Kristallnacht (9–10 November 1938)

On 7 November 1938, a 17-year-old Polish Jew, Herschel Grynszpan, went into the German embassy in Paris, randomly picked a German, Ernst vom Rath, and shot him. Grynszpan was angry at the Germans for the way they had treated his parents. Seriously wounded, vom Rath was rushed to hospital.

On 8 November, Joseph Goebbels, the Nazi Minister for Propaganda, used the incident to stir up trouble against Jews in Germany.

- He ordered the local papers in Hanover, Grynszpan's home town, to print articles condemning the Paris shooting.
- He also used the SA, SS and Gestapo to attack local synagogues and the houses of local Jews.
- Then things escalated. On 9 November, vom Rath died.

Hitler gets involved

Goebbels told Hitler the news on the afternoon of 9 November. They agreed to turn the violence against Jews in Hanover into a nationwide attack. Nazi leaders were encouraged to arrange attacks on Jews and their property, but were told to do so under cover. Police were told not prevent any violence against Jews by members of the public. Instructions were also sent to local SS groups to arrest as many Jews as the prisons could take.

The violence on 9–10 November

On 9 and 10 November, gangs smashed and burned Jewish property and attacked Jews. An example of the violence included one 18-year-old Jew being thrown from a third floor window. Some gangs were in Nazi uniforms. Others were SA and Hitler Youth. They were told not to wear uniforms, so that the violence would seem to be by the general public.

Some Germans were horrified; others watched with pleasure or joined in. Official figures – which underestimate the damage – listed 814 shops, 171 homes and 191 synagogues destroyed. Furthermore, about 100 Jews were killed. The damage was so bad that these events were called *Kristallnacht* (Crystal Night) or the Night of Broken Glass.

Source G

A British newspaper, the *Daily Telegraph*, reporting on 12 November 1938.

```
Mob law ruled in Berlin... as hordes of
hooligans went on an orgy of destruction.
I have never seen an anti-Jewish outbreak
as sickening... fashionably dressed women
clapped their hands screaming with glee
[and] held up their children to see the
'fun'. No attempt was made by the police to
stop the rioters.
```

The aftermath

Goebbels blamed the Jews for starting the trouble on *Kristallnacht* and announced they would be punished.

- Jews were fined 1 billion marks to pay for the damage.
- By 12 November, 20,000 Jews had been rounded up and sent to concentration camps.

Interpretation 1

From *The Third Reich in Power*, by Richard J. Evans published in 2006.

The violence [during *Kristallnacht*] was familiar from the behaviour of the brownshirts in 1933. But this time it went much further. It was clearly more widespread and more destructive. It demonstrated the hatred of the Jews now gripped not only the stormtroopers and [Nazi] party activists but was spreading to other parts of the population – above all to the young, upon whom five years of Nazism in schools and the Hitler Youth had clearly had an effect.

Interpretation 2

From *Life in Germany*, by Steve Waugh, published in 2009.

This led to Kristallnacht, so called because of the thousands of Jewish shop windows which were smashed... Many Germans watched the events with alarm and concern. However, the Nazi-controlled press presented it as a reaction of ordinary Germans against Jews. Most Germans did not believe this, but hardly anyone protested for fear of arrest and death.

Activities ?

1   Who suffered most under the Nazis, 1933–39? Write an opinion in notes and then explain your opinion to your class.

2   Look at the timeline you produced in response to Activity 3 on page 132. Write a paragraph to explain why 1933, 1935 and 1938 are key dates in the Nazi persecution of the Jews.

3   As a whole class, discuss why there was so little opposition to the persecution of the Jews from members of the public in Nazi Germany. Afterwards, write a paragraph to outline your own views.

The climax of peacetime persecution

In January 1939, the Nazis decided to evict all Jews from Germany. The Reich Office for Jewish Emigration was set up under Reinhard Heydrich, head of the Gestapo. His task was to deport Germany's Jews.

To achieve this, in April 1939, orders went out that all Jews should be evicted from their homes and collected together for deportation. This was how things stood when the Second World War broke out in September 1939.

The role of the German people

The Nazi government kept some atrocities against Jews secret. However, most of what happened to Jews between 1933 and 1939 was known, both within Germany and in other countries. Indeed, many Germans took part in the persecution and many others – and most other countries – did little to stop it. This is difficult to understand.

As we have seen, people who criticised the Nazis were severely dealt with. Some Germans may therefore have been too scared to oppose it. Others convinced themselves that the suffering inflicted on Jews was not real – or just ignored it entirely. But many Germans seem to have become convinced by ideas at the time that persecution of the Jews was justified, so they supported it and even took part in it.

Extend your knowledge

The bigger picture
The persecution of minorities was worse during the Second World War, which started in 1939. As German troops defeated countries all over Europe, the Nazis became responsible for even more Jews. By the end of the Second World War, it is estimated that the Nazis had murdered 200,000 'gypsies' and six million Jews in concentration camps.

Exam-style question, Section B

How far do you agree with Interpretation 1 about the events of *Kristallnacht* in 1938?

Explain your answer, using Interpretations 1 and 2 (page 136) and your own knowledge of the historical context. **16 marks**

Exam tip

Good answers will create an argument, setting out:

- how far you agree with Interpretation 1, with evidence to support your view

- how far you disagree with Interpretation 1, again with evidence to support your view.

Evidence should come from Interpretation 1 or 2 and your own knowledge.

Marks are given for good spelling, punctuation, grammar and specialist historical terminology.

THINKING HISTORICALLY Cause and Consequence (6a)

Seeing things differently

Different times and places have different sets of ideas. Beliefs about how the world works, how human societies should be governed or the best way to achieve economic prosperity can all be radically different from our own. It is important for the historian to take into account these different attitudes when examining people's reactions and motivations in the past.

Nazi persecution of the Jews

During the years 1933–39, the German government officially called Jews vermin, ruined their businesses, robbed them of German citizenship, banned them from most jobs, destroyed their property, imprisoned them and violently assaulted them.

1   Imagine that the current government of Britain treated Jews like that today.

   a   What would be the reaction of the British Parliament?

   b   What would be the reaction of the Jews?

   c   What would be the reaction of the press and the general public?

2   Attitudes in Nazi Germany towards Jews were different from current attitudes in Britain.

   a   Write one sentence explaining the attitude of the Nazis towards Jews in the 1930s. Write one sentence explaining the attitude of the British government towards Jews today.

   b   Write one sentence explaining the attitudes in German society towards the persecution of Jews in the 1930s. Write one sentence explaining the attitudes in British society towards the persecution of Jews today.

3   Write a paragraph explaining how attitudes in Germany towards Jews in the 1930s contributed to the persecution of the Jews under the Nazis. Remember to refer to both the attitude of the government and the attitude of ordinary people.

Summary

- Treatment of minority groups was shaped by eugenics, racial hygiene and anti-Semitism.
- The Slavs, 'gypsies', homosexuals and people with disabilities were all mistreated.
- Nazi persecution of Jews began in 1933, became worse in 1935, with the Nuremberg Laws, and then became worse still from 1938 after *Kristallnacht*.

Checkpoint

Strengthen

S1 Describe Nazi beliefs about eugenics, racial hygiene and anti-Semitism.

S2 In what ways did the Nazis mistreat minority groups in Germany?

S3 Describe mistreatment of Jews in 1933, the Nuremberg Laws and *Kristallnacht*.

Challenge

C1 Explain Nazi reasoning behind their persecution of minority groups and Jews.

C2 Explain why few Germans seem to have actively opposed the persecution of Jews.

How confident do you feel about your answers to these questions? If you are unsure, look again at pages 131–132 for S1, pages 133–134 for S2 and pages 134–137 for S3. For C1 and C2, discuss with other people in class. Your teacher can provide hints.

Recap quiz

1 What laws did the Nazis introduce to encourage marriage, motherhood and childbirth?
2 What Nazi youth groups were there for young German girls and boys?
3 What does KdF stand for?
4 What is 'invisible' unemployment?
5 Name the Nazi organisations which affected the standard of living of workers.
6 When did the Nazi boycott of Jewish shops begin?
7 When were the Nuremberg Laws passed?
8 Which law forbade the marriage of Jews to Germans?
9 What event caused the beginning of *Kristallnacht*?
10 How many Jews were arrested and taken to concentration camps by 12 November after *Kristallnacht*?

Activities

1 Match up the following lists:

a	Eugenics is	i	anti-Jewish views
b	Racial hygiene is	ii	the study of selective breeding
c	Herrenvolk means	iii	unworthy of life
d	Untermenschen means	iv	the master race
e	Lebensunwertes means	v	choosing parents for racial purity
f	Anti-Semitism means	vii	sub-humans

2 Decide whether each of these statements is true or false.

   a The Slavs were an ancient tribe who settled in Europe.
   b Slav people, such as the Poles, occupied land that Hitler wanted for German *Lebensraum*.
   c 'Gypsies' was the name the Nazis used for the Roma people.
   d There were two million 'gypsies' in Germany in 1933.
   e 'Gypsies' were often sent to concentration camps for being 'undesirables'.
   f From 1936 some 'gypsies' were made to live in special camps.
   g 5,000 homosexuals died in Nazi concentration camps.
   h Nazi laws encouraged the voluntary castration of homosexuals.
   i In 1933, the Nazis made it compulsory for the blind and deaf to be sterilised.
   j From 1939, the Nazis had a policy of killing disabled children, called the T4 programme.

3 Which one of the following was NOT a reason why few Germans objected to the persecution of Jews?

   a Fear
   b Propaganda
   c Turning a blind eye
   d Ignorance of what was happening
   e Too self-centred to care

Explaining why historians' interpretations differ

In Paper 3, one question will ask you to suggest one reason why two interpretations give different views about an aspect of your study. To understand the reasons for difference you need to appreciate that historians writing about any society have to make choices and they have to make judgements. They choose what to concentrate on. They also come to views about the topics they research. Historians may be focusing on different aspects, using different sources, or reaching different conclusions on the same sources. These factors explain reasons for difference.

Historians focus on different things

Interpretations of history are created by historians. Historians construct interpretations based on evidence from the past. Think of their role as similar to a house-builder: the evidence – the sources available - are the building blocks for their construction. Historians choose what enquiries to make of the materials available to them. No historian can write about the whole of history everywhere. What shapes the historian's work is what they want to explore and what they choose to focus on. Figure 1 below lists some of the choices they make:

Place	National History	Local History
Period	One century or more	One decade or less
Range	Overview	Depth
People	National Leaders	Ordinary people
Aspect	Political history	Social history

Figure 1 Some examples of historians' choices.

Figure 2 The historian's focus.

After choosing their focus, the historian must find evidence to pursue their enquiry. So, they will be looking for different things in order to answer different questions about the past.

Historians A and B below are both writing about the same school, but their focus is different. In looking at the history of a school, several different enquiries are possible, for example the focus could be on the building, the curriculum, students' achievements and so on. As you read the interpretations below, identify what the two historians are interested in – what have their enquiries focused on?

Historian A

The village school has been in continuous use since 1870. It continues to educate local children from the ages of 5–11. They are educated in the same building that was constructed in 1870. Its outward appearance has hardly changed. It was originally built of red brick, with white-painted wooden doors and the large windows that can still be seen today. The schoolroom windows, reaching almost to the high celling, were designed to give plenty of light, but with windowsills too high for students to be distracted by being able to see anything outside. Although a modern extension at the rear was added in the 1960s, the key features of the school building represent a remarkable degree of continuity in education in the locality.

Historian B

Education locally has changed in the period since 1870. Lessons in the 19th century focused almost entirely on the 3Rs of reading, writing and arithmetic. There was much learning by heart and copying out of passages. By the 21st century, the wall displays and the students' exercise books show that science, history, geography, have all become important parts of the curriculum and with more emphasis on finding out and creativity. In terms of the curriculum, the degree of change in education since 1870 has been considerable.

Read each of the statements about Historians A and B below.

a The historians have different views about the amount of change in education in the village.

b One of the historians is wrong.

c One of the historians is biased.

d They are just giving different opinions.

e They have used different evidence.

f They have focused on different aspects.

g They are both correct in their conclusions.

h They have emphasised different things.

i They are looking for different things.

j The historians disagree.

k The historians do not disagree.

1 Make a list of each of the statements you agree with and another list with those that you do not agree with.

2 Explain why Historians A and B have different views about the extent to which education has changed in the village. Try to use words form the box below in your answer:

focus	emphasis	aspect	evidence	conclusions	enquiry	interested

Historians reach different conclusions from the evidence

Even when historians have the same focus and purpose – for example, even if they both seek to explain why the same thing happened – their conclusions may still be different. This is because the evidence from the past doesn't provide us with an answer: historians have to work out an answer from it – and often the evidence points in different directions. Then, the historians have to make judgments. Differences may arise because:

- they have given weight to different sources
- they have reached different conclusions on the same sources.

In a court of law, every member of the jury hears the same evidence, but they sometimes disagree about their verdict. It comes down to making judgments about what conclusions can be drawn from the evidence.

Activity   ?

Study Interpretations X & X on page XX.

Which of the following reasons explains why the views in interpretations X and X are different? Make a list of all those that you think apply. You can add other reasons of your own if you wish.

a The historians are interested in different aspects of the topic.

b The historians have emphasised different things when giving their views.

c The evidence from the period points in different directions.

d The historians have reached conclusions by giving weight to different sources from the period.

Choose one reason you have listed and write one or two sentences to explain why you chose it. Remember to use the interpretations in your answer. Refer to sources from the period too, if you listed reason c or d.

Summary

- What shapes the historian's work is which aspect of history the historian chooses to explore.
- Historians' judgements differ because the evidence can support different views. They may reach different conclusions because they have given weight to different sources or because they are looking at different aspects of the topic.

Preparing for your GCSE Paper 3 exam

Paper 3 overview

Your Paper 3 is in two sections that examine the Modern Depth Study. In Section A, you answer one question on a source and one using your own knowledge. Section B is a case study using sources and interpretations of history, and the four questions will be about the same issue. The paper is worth 30% of your History assessment.

History Paper 3	Modern Depth Study		Time 1 hour 20 minutes
Section A	Answer 2 questions	16 marks	20 minutes
Section B	Answer 4 questions	32 marks + 4 for SPaG	60 minutes

Modern Depth Option 31 Weimar and Nazi Germany 1918–39

Section A

You will answer Questions 1 and 2.

1 Give two things you can infer from Source A about... (4 marks)

Source A is on the question paper. You should work out two inferences from it. An inference is something not directly stated in the source, but which you can support using details from it.

You have a table to complete for each inference: 'What I can infer. . .' and 'Details in the source that tell me this'. Allow five minutes to read the source and to write your answer. This question is only worth four marks and you should keep the answer brief and not try to put more information on extra lines.

2 Explain why... (12 marks)

This question asks you to explain the reasons why something happened. Allow 15 minutes to write your answer. You are given two information points as prompts to help you. You do not have to use the prompts and you will not lose marks by leaving them out. Always remember to add in a new point of your own as well: higher marks are gained by adding in a

point extra to the prompts. You will be given at least two pages of lines in the answer booklet for your answer. This does not mean you should try to fill all the space. The front page of the exam paper tells you 'there may be more space than you need'. Aim to write an answer giving at least three explained reasons.

Section B

You will answer Question 3 (a), (b), (c) and (d). All four questions will be about the same issue. Question (a) will be based on contemporary sources (evidence from the period you are studying). Questions (b) (c) and (d) will be based on two historical interpretations.

3(a) How useful are Sources A and B for an enquiry into... (8 marks)

You are given two sources to evaluate. They are in a separate sources booklet so you can keep them in front of you while you write your answer. Allow 15 minutes for this question to give yourself time to read both sources carefully. Make sure your answer deals with both sources and use your knowledge when you evaluate the source. For example, you could use it to evaluate the accuracy or completeness of the evidence.

You should make a judgement about the usefulness of each source, giving clear reasons. Only choose points which are directly relevant to the enquiry in the question. You should always take account of the provenance (the nature, origin and purpose) of the source when you think about the usefulness of the information it gives. How reliable is it?

3(b) Study Interpretations 1 and 2. They give different views about...

What is the main difference between these views? (4 marks)

Allow ten minutes for this question to give yourself time to read the extracts. Identify an overall difference rather than different pieces of information. For example, think about whether one is positive and the other negative. Then use details from both interpretations. The difference is… this is shown because Interpretation 1 says…, …, but Interpretation 2 says… …

3(c) Suggest one reason why Interpretations 1 and 2 give different views about... (4 marks)

Allow five minutes for this question. It does not need a long answer (it is only worth four marks) and you have already read the interpretations, but you will need to use both extracts again and perhaps Sources B and C. Give a clear reason for the difference. One reason could be because the historians have chosen to give weight to different evidence. If you use this reason, you should use both Sources B and C to show that the evidence from the period differs. If you use other reasons, for example about what the historian is focusing on, you will not need to use Sources B and C.

3(d) How far do you agree with Interpretation [1 or 2] about...? (16 marks + 4 marks SPaG)

This question, including SPaG, is worth 20 marks – over one-third of your marks for the whole of the Modern Depth Study. Make sure you have kept 30 minutes of the exam time to answer it and to check your spelling, punctuation and grammar. You will already have worked out the views in the two interpretations for Question (b). Question (d) asks you how far you agree with the view in one of them. Plan your answer before you begin to write, and put your points in two columns: For and Against. You should use points from the two interpretations and also use your own contextual knowledge. Think about it as if you were putting weight on each side to decide what your judgement is going to be for the conclusion. That way your whole answer hangs together – it is coherent. Be clear about your reasons (your criteria) for your judgement.

In this question, four extra marks will be gained for good spelling, punctuation and grammar. Use sentences, paragraphs, capital letters, commas and full stops, etc. Try also to use relevant specialist terms – for example, terms such as constitution, communism, legislation.

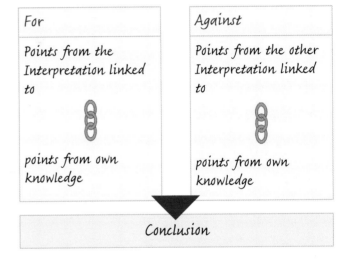

Paper 3, Section A: Question 1

Study Source A on page 100.
Give **two** things you can infer from Source A about how Hitler kept power.
Complete the table below to explain your answer. **(4 marks)**

Average answer

What I can infer:
Germany had suffered many severe problems, which Hitler helped to solve.

Details in the source that tell me this:
The Treaty of Versailles was unfair and unemployment went up in the Depression.

The inference is correct, but the detail given to support it is not from the source.

Verdict

This is an average response because an inference is made, but without appropriate support. Use the feedback to rewrite this answer, making as many improvements as you can.

Strong answer

What I can infer:
Germany had suffered many severe problems, which Hitler helped to solve.

Details in the source that tell me this:
Source says that Hitler 'saved his country from utter despondency and degradation'.

Details are given that support a correct inference.

Verdict

This is a strong response because an inference is made and supported by the source.

Paper 3, Section A: Question 2

Explain why unemployment fell in Germany between 1933 and 1939. You may use the following in your answer:

- National Labour Service (RAD)
- autobahns.

You **must** also use information of your own. (**12 marks**)

Exam tip

Focus on explaining 'why'. Aim to give at least three clear reasons.

Average answer

The National Labour Service (RAD) paid people for doing public works, like planting trees and draining marshes. At first, the RAD was voluntary. But from 1935, it was compulsory. Workers wore uniforms, lived in camps and did military drills and parades as well as working.

Work on autobahns also made unemployment fall. [Details follow describing the building of autobahns.] Hitler introduced conscription in Germany in 1935. Hitler's armed forces needed armaments and vehicles and uniforms, so this was a boost to Germany's industries, like the arms industry, coal and iron and steel and textiles.

Overall, the factors of new jobs and conscription explain why unemployment fell in Germany.

The stimulus factor provided in the question (the RAD) is used. Accurate detail about the RAD is given, but there is no attempt to relate this factor to the question (how the RAD reduced unemployment). The details given are not well chosen – for example, there is no information about how many people worked for the RAD or how much this reduced unemployment.

Answer includes own factor (conscription) and there is some detailed information given. But there is no line of argument here relating to the question.

Answer attempts to address the question directly, but the point is not developed.

Verdict

This is an average answer because:

- it includes some detailed knowledge, including a factor from own knowledge
- there is no sustained line of reasoning running through the whole answer which explains why all these factors reduced unemployment
- the detailed knowledge chosen is not the most relevant. For example, there are no details to show how many jobs each factor provided.

Use the feedback to rewrite this answer, making as many improvements as you can.

Paper 3, Section A: Question 2

Explain why unemployment fell in Germany between 1933 and 1939. (**12 marks**)

Strong answer

Unemployment fell in Germany from five million in 1933 to half a million in 1939. There were several factors explaining why unemployment fell.

One reason unemployment fell was the National Labour Service (RAD). The RAD paid unemployed people to do public works, like planting trees and draining marshes. At first people volunteered for the RAD. However, from 1935 it was compulsory for all young men to work for six months in the RAD. This meant that none of the people in the RAD counted as unemployed. Numbers in the RAD grew to 422,000, so this cut unemployment by almost half a million. This makes it an important reason why unemployment fell.

[Paragraph on autobahns, explaining how many people worked on the autobahns and how this gave work to the unemployed.]

Hitler introduced conscription in Germany in 1935. By 1939, there were 1,360,000 people in the armed forces. These all needed armaments, vehicles and uniforms, so this was a boost to Germany's industries, like the arms industry, coal, iron, steel, and textiles. Employment in the aircraft industry alone grew from 4,000 to over 70,000.

One further reason why official unemployment figures fell 1933–1939 was 'invisible unemployment'. From 1933, women were banned from professional jobs as teachers, doctors and civil servants. By 1934, 350,000 women had given up work. These women were not counted as unemployed. From April 1933, Jews were banned from government jobs and many Jewish civil servants and teachers were sacked, too. These people were not included in the unemployment figures either. So, removing people from jobs and then not counting them as unemployed was another reason why unemployment figures in Germany fell 1933–1939.

Overall, several factors explain why unemployment actually fell in Germany. The RAD and autobahns helped. Conscription boosted other industries and it kept over a million people off unemployment figures. Additionally, invisible unemployment reduced the numbers officially unemployed.

Introduction shows good knowledge of the period and uses the words in the question to start the answer.

The answer relates one stimulus factor (the RAD) to the question. It also consistently keeps up the argument, always saying throughout the paragraph how the RAD reduced unemployment. The choice of information is accurate and relevant to the question.

Introduces own factor (conscription). Consistently answers the question, giving accurate and relevant detail to support their argument.

The conclusion rounds off a good structure for the answer.

Verdict

This is a strong answer because:

- it gives an analysis of the factors which caused unemployment to fall
- it includes the stimulus and factors from own knowledge
- it consistently sustains an argument throughout the answer
- it uses detailed, accurate and relevant information to support the argument.

Paper 3, Section B: Question 3a

Study Sources C and D on pages 69–70.

How useful are Sources C and D for an enquiry into the way Hitler came to power?

Explain your answer, using Sources C and D and your own knowledge of the historical context.

(8 marks)

Exam tip

Consider the strengths and weaknesses of the evidence. Your evaluation must link to the enquiry and use contextual knowledge. Your reasons (criteria) for judgement should be clear. Include points about:

- what information is relevant and what you can infer from the source
- how does the provenance (nature, origin, purpose) of each source affect its usefulness?

Average answer

Source C is useful because it mentions how Brüning kept issuing commands but he was not obeyed. This shows that the existing government could not solve Germany's problems, so people wanted to turn to somebody else.

> A relevant section of the source is quoted and the answer tells us how it would be useful for this enquiry. Inferences are made but not developed.

Source C is also useful because it shows that Germany was in chaos. Unemployment was at five million by 1932 and this caused street violence like Source C says, so Germany needed a strong hand like Hitler. But Source C is a story, so we can't be sure that it is describing how things really were.

> The idea that Germany was in chaos and needed a strong hand, like Hitler, is valid inference, but needs to be developed. Provenance of the source is mentioned, but only very briefly.

Source D is useful. It shows that Hitler needed the help of two other people to lift him to power. It comes from a political magazine, so it shows a political point of view about Hitler coming to power.

> A valid point, but it needs more detail. It starts to discuss the importance of the provenance, but needs to develop this idea.

Verdict

This is an average answer because:

- it has taken relevant information from both sources, used inference to show how a source can be useful and mentioned provenance (so it is not a weak answer)
- it has begun to show how the sources could be used for the enquiry, including using inference, but these points are not sufficiently developed
- the importance of provenance to evaluate the sources needs developing.

Use the feedback to rewrite this answer, making as many improvements as you can.

Paper 3, Section B: Question 3a

How useful are Sources C and D for an enquiry into the way Hitler came to power?
Explain your answer, using Sources C and D and your own knowledge of the historical context. **(8 marks)**

Strong answer

S Source C is useful because it mentions how Brüning kept issuing commands but he was not obeyed. It is accurate because we know that Brüning issued 66 decrees in 1932 and this source shows why this helped Hitler come to power. It says 'each week there were new decrees'. I can infer from this that people were getting fed up with decrees which achieved nothing and wanted an alternative.

Source C is also useful because it shows that Germany was in chaos, which helps to explain how Hitler came to power. I know, from my own knowledge, that the impression Source C gives is an accurate one. Unemployment was at five million in Germany by 1932 and this caused street violence like the source says. Many people in Germany thought that Germany needed a strong hand like Hitler. Source C is therefore useful; it gives us extra detail about the violence and explains what German people wanted – as Source C puts it, 'a man with hair on his chest'.

Source C was written by a British journalist. In one way this weakens how useful it is. The journalist tells us what Germans thought – 'hate in their heads', for example. But he was not German, he couldn't really know what they thought. On the other hand, he writes from first-hand experience. He tells us exactly what he saw – the knives on the streets, the bloodshed – that we know took place. Therefore the impression he gives of the attitude of many Germans is also very believable – 'Brüning is weak', 'the Nazis will be in power by Christmas'. This is reliable information about what people were doing and saying and makes the source useful. Even if it is a story, it seems to be trying to create an accurate impression.

Source D is useful. It shows that political commentators at the time thought that Hitler needed the help of Hindenburg and von Papen to lift him to power, and that they were reluctant to do it. This idea is supported by von Papen's comment to Hindenburg at the time, when he said "we will push Hitler so far into a corner, he will squeak like a mouse". The source is from a British magazine, which concentrated on political events, so it gives us an informed view about Hitler coming to power and suggests that the role of Hindenburg and von Papen was widely known as it was portrayed in this way in a magazine designed for the British public. This makes it more useful.

This is a well-developed point. The content of the source, inference from the source other knowledge are all combined to show how the source is useful in explaining the circumstances behind Hitler's rise to power.

Content of the source and specific knowledge used to show how the source throws light on Hitler's rise to power.

This is a balanced view of the provenance of the source, which makes a reasonable case for its usefulness.

Answer uses provenance to decide that the source is useful and then compares its content with own knowledge to show how the source helps us to understand Hitler's rise.

Verdict

This is a strong answer because:

- it has analysed both sources, making inferences from them
- it has used contextual knowledge in the evaluation of both sources
- evaluation takes provenance into account and explains why they are useful.

Paper 3, Section B: Questions 3b-c

Study Interpretations 1 and 2 on page 153. They give different views about the way Hitler came to power.
What is the main difference between these views?
Explain your answer, using details from both interpretations.
(4 marks)

Exam tip

Remember to identify a main difference and then use details from both interpretations to support your answer.

Average answer

A main difference is that Interpretation 1 emphasises the view that the social and political chaos in Germany was the reason Hitler came to power. Interpretation 2 says that von Papen and Hindenburg were the reason. It says 'Von Papen convinced President Hindenburg that a coalition with Hitler would save Germany'.

A valid difference is identified but no details are given from Interpretation 1.

Verdict

This is an average answer because it identifies a difference, with some detail from Interpretation 2, but it does not use detail from Interpretation 1 to support the difference.
Use the feedback to rewrite this answer, making as many improvements as you can.

Suggest one reason why Interpretations 1 and 2 give different views about how Hitler came to power.
You may use Sources C and D on pages 69–70 to help explain your answer. **(4 marks)**

Exam tip

Give a clear reason. If you decide to use Sources C and D, choose details from them to show that the historians may have given weight to different sources.

Average answer

The interpretations may differ because the historians have given weight to different sources. For example, Source C describes the political weakness of Brüning and the social unrest in Germany and says that was why Hitler became more popular. That supports Interpretation 1, which emphasises the political weakness of Brüning and the Reichstag in explaining why the Nazis became the biggest party.

A reason is given and Source C is used, but nothing is said about Interpretation 2.

Verdict

This is an average answer because it gives a reason for the different views with support from Source C, but Source D has not been used.

Use the feedback to rewrite this answer, making as many improvements as you can.

Paper 3, Section B: Questions 3b–c

Study Interpretations 1 and 2. They give different views about how Hitler came to power.
What is the main difference between these views?
Explain your answer, using details from both interpretations. **(4 marks)**

Strong answer

A main difference is that Interpretation 1 emphasises the view that the social and political chaos in Germany was the reason Hitler came to power. It says that businesses collapsed and unemployment went up and that democracy was replaced by dictatorship and that, as a result, more people showed an interest in Hitler.

On the other hand, Interpretation 2 says that von Papen and Hindenburg were the reason. It says 'von Papen convinced President Hindenburg that a coalition with Hitler would save Germany'.

Details from both Interpretation 1 and Interpretation 2 explain the main difference between the two views.

Verdict

This is a strong answer because it identifies a valid difference with support from both interpretations.

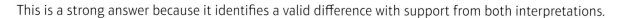

Suggest **one** reason why Interpretations 1 and 2 give different views about Hitler's rise to power.
You may use Sources C and D on pages 69–70 to help explain your answer. **(4 marks)**

Strong answer

The interpretations may differ because the historians have given weight to different sources. For example, Source C describes the political weakness of Brüning and the social unrest in Germany and says that was why Hitler became more popular. That supports Interpretation 1, which emphasises the political weakness of Brüning and the Reichstag in explaining why the Nazis became the biggest party.

On the other hand, Source D, which suggests that it was plotting by people like von Papen and Hindenburg that 'lifted' Hitler to power on their shoulders, provides support for the emphasis on their roles in Interpretation 2.

Details from Source C are used to show support for Interpretation 1 AND details from Source D are used to support Interpretation 2.

Verdict

This is a strong answer because it gives a valid reason for the different views and supports it using both sources.

Paper 3, Section B: Question 3d

Up to 4 marks of the total for this question will be awarded for spelling, punctuation, grammar and use of specialist terminology.

How far do you agree with Interpretation 1 about the way Hitler came to power?

Explain your answer, using both interpretations and your knowledge of the historical context. **(20 marks)**

Average answer

Interpretation 1 says that there was a depression in Germany and that this caused problems. It also says that the politicians couldn't solve these problems so people showed interest in Hitler's ideas and voted for Nazi representatives.

From my own knowledge I know that unemployment went up to five million in 1932 and that Hitler got 13 million votes in the presidential election.

But Interpretation 1 does not explain how Hitler became Chancellor. It says people supported Hitler and the Nazis but there were no elections for the Chancellor so the people could not choose him. The Chancellor had to be chosen by President Hindenburg. Interpretation 2 explains how Hindenburg decided to choose Hitler as Chancellor so I am more likely to support the view in Interpretation 2 than Interpretation 1.

Relevant details from Interpretation 1 are used and the student's own knowledge is included. However, the knowledge is simply added on to the extract. The answer should explain clearly whether the information supports or challenges the view.

Relevant details are chosen to contrast Interpretation 1 with Interpretation 2 and own knowledge is added in. A judgement is given, but this is not fully explained, with details.

Verdict

This is an average answer because:

- it includes relevant details from both the interpretations and contextual knowledge, so it is not a weak answer
- it does not give enough detail to justify the conclusion for it to be a strong answer
- spelling is accurate and there is some use of specialist terms (e.g. presidential election), but this is not wide-ranging and punctuation is limited to the use of full stops.

Use the feedback to rewrite this answer, making as many improvements as you can.

Paper 3, Section B: Question 3d

How far do you agree with Interpretation 1 about Hitler's rise to power?
Explain your answer, using both interpretations and your knowledge of the historical context. **(20 marks)**

Strong answer

Interpretation 1 says that there was a depression in Germany between 1929 and 1933 and that this caused economic problems, like failing businesses, and social problems, like unemployment. From my own knowledge, I know that unemployment reached five million, so Interpretation 1 is correct. It also says that the moderate parties in the Reichstag couldn't agree how to solve these problems. I know that this is true; it resulted in Brüning using Article 48 66 times in 1932 because the Reichstag could not agree what to do.

Interpretation 1 goes on to say that all this caused support for Hitler's ideas. This is true, because Hitler got 13 million votes in the presidential election. So I would give some support for the view in Interpretation 1. Interpretation 2, on the other hand, does not explain how Hitler got to such a strong position that Hindenburg was persuaded to choose him as Chancellor. Interpretation 2 is weak in aspect, which is another reason why I am tempted to support the view in Interpretation 1.

But Interpretation 1 does not explain how Hitler became Chancellor. It explains how Hitler received support in the Presidential elections, and how the NSDAP became the biggest party in the Reichstag, but there were no elections for the Chancellor so the people could not choose him. The Chancellor had to be chosen by President Hindenburg. This is an important issue because I know from my own knowledge that Hindenburg thought Hitler was a 'jumped-up corporal'. So why did he choose him? This is the key reason why I support Interpretation 2. Interpretation 2 explains how von Papen persuaded Hindenburg that coalition with Hitler would save Germany from revolution and that Hitler could be safely controlled. This is the key reason Hitler became Chancellor, so it is the reason I support the view in Interpretation 2 more than Interpretation 1.

In one sense I agree with both interpretations. Interpretation 1 explains how Hitler came to be in a position to be chosen as Chancellor. Interpretation 2 explains why he WAS chosen to be Chancellor. Interpretation 1 can only tell me about the general situation in Germany at the time. It doesn't speak directly about Hitler in particular. Interpretation 2 is much more specific for this enquiry – why did Hitler come to power. Interpretation 2 tells me much more directly why Hitler came to power. So, on balance, I agree with Interpretation 2 more than Interpretation 1.

The extracts are analysed to show contrasting views and contextual knowledge is integrated.

A key issue is identified and there is good use of contextual knowledge to make a judgement.

Both views are considered and a judgement is reached with a clear reason. Knowledge is used well to support the judgement. Appropriate specialist terminology is used (economic and social, moderate parties, Article 48, Chancellor, NSDAP).

Verdict

This is a strong answer because:

- both interpretations are analysed and evaluated using own knowledge
- the line of reasoning is coherent and the judgement is appropriately justified with a clear reason
- SPaG demonstrates accuracy, effective control of meaning and the use of a wide range of specialist terms.

Interpretations Booklet

Interpretation 1

From *Weimar and Nazi Germany*, by Stephen Lee (1996).

… between 1929 and 1933 crisis returned in full force. Germany experienced a serious depression. This caused the collapse of businesses and an increase in unemployment. The moderate parties of the Weimar Republic could not agree… More use was made of Article 48. The Reichstag was by-passed. Democracy was replaced by dictatorship. A larger part of the population showed interest in Hitler's ideas. The result was that the Nazis became the biggest party in the Reichstag. [They] gave Hitler power, hoping he would use it as they wanted.

Interpretation 2

From *Nazi Germany 1930–39*, by Steve Waugh and John Wright (2007).

Von Papen was determined to regain power. He met Hitler and agreed that Hitler would lead a government with von Papen as the Vice-Chancellor. Intrigue took the place of open political debate. The landowners and leaders of industry were convinced that von Papen and Hitler were saving Germany from Schleicher's military take-over. Von Papen convinced President Hindenburg that a coalition with Hitler would save Germany. Von Papen said that he could control Hitler. On 30 January, Adolf Hitler became Chancellor of Germany.

Answers to Germany Recap Questions

Chapter 1

1 Friedrich Ebert
2 SPD
3 Paul von Hindenburg
4 Gustav Stresemann
5 1929
6 Reichsrat
7 21
8 Chancellor
9 This part of the constitution said that, in a crisis, the chancellor could ask the president to pass a necessary law, by decree, without the support of the Reichstag
10 KPD, SPD, DDP, ZP, DVP, DNVP, NSDAP

Chapter 2

1 German Workers' Party
2 National Socialist German Workers' Party
3 A Nazi newspaper
4 Hitler's own personal bodyguard
5 A violent uprising intended to overthrow existing leaders
6 Paul von Hindenburg
7 Heinrich Bruning
8 Franz von Papen
9 Kurt von Schleicher
10 Adolf Hitler

Chapter 3

1 27 February 1933
2 23 March 1933
3 30 June 1934
4 Heinrich Himmler
5 Reinhard Heydrich
6 Joseph Goebbels
7 A way of controlling art and culture so it was consistent with Nazi ideas
8 Martin Niemöller
9 The Edelweiss Pirates
10 The Swing Youth

Chapter 4

1 The Law for the Encouragement of Marriage, 1933, and divorce laws to encourage childbirth.
2 Little Fellows, German Young People,   Hitler Youth; Young Maidens, League of German Maidens.
3 Strength Through Joy
4 The Nazis found ways to reduce the number of people recorded as unemployed. The real number of unemployed people was higher than the official figures.
5 The Labour Front (DAF)Blood
6 1933
7 1936
8 The Reich Law for the Protection of German Blood and Honour20,000
9 Herschel Grynszpan's murder of Ernst vom Rath
10 20,000

Index

Acknowledgements

Picture Credits

The publisher would like to thank the following for their kind permission to reproduce their photographs:

(Key: b-bottom; c-centre; l-left; r-right; t-top)

Alamy Images: CBW 134, Chronicle 7t, 11, 76, Chronicle 7t, 11, 76, Granger, NYC. 13, Heritage Image Partnership Ltd 37l, Hi-Story 8, 17, INTERFOTO 19, 74, 95, Trinity Mirror / Mirrorpix 94, World History Archive 24; **Bridgeman Art Library Ltd:** Carl von Ossietzky as an internee at Esterwegen concentration camp, Oldenburg, after 28th February 1935 / SZ Photo 86, Farming Family from Kalenberg, 1939, Wissel, Adolf (1894-1973) / Property of the Federal Republic of German 109, German Poster urging the public to vote for Hindenburg, 1932, German School / Private Collection / Peter Newark Military Pictures 68, Germany raises the tombstone of the Treaty of Versailles, illustration from Kladderadatsch, 1926, Garvens, Oskar Theodor (1874-1951) / Bibliotheque Nationale, Paris, France / Archives Charmet 29, 'Grosstadt' (urban debauchery) 1927-28 (triptych), Dix, Otto (1891-1969) / Staatsgalerie, Stuttgart, Germany 37r, Hitler's SS troops parade with Nazi standards on Party Day at Nuremberg, 1933, German School / Private Collection / Peter Newark Military Pictures 42, 56, Joseph Goebbels addressing the Nazi Party Congress, Nuremberg, 1936, German Photographer / Private Collection / Look and Learn / Elgar Collection 91, Munich Putsch, 1940, Schmitt, H. / Private Collection / Peter Newark Pictures 51, Poster advertising the KDF-Wagen (Volkswagen), 1939, German School / Private Collection / Archives Charmet 129, The Last Blow! 1933, German School / Private Collection / Peter Newark Pictures 88, The Progression of Hitler', illustration from Simplicissimus, 1924, Schilling, E. / Bibliotheque Nationale, Paris, France / Archives Charmet 52, Time and again we see the Fuhrer surrounded by children. Baldur von Schirach stands to the right, from 'Adolf Hitler: Bilder aus dem Leben des Fuhrers' published in 1935, Hoffmann, Heinrich (1885-1957) / Private Collection / The Stapleton Collection 114, What does Spartacus want?' Spartacist League poster, German School / Kunstgewerbe Museum, Zurich, Switzerland / Archives Charmet 21; **Daily Express:** BCA 78; **Getty Images:** Bettmann 14, 23, 124, Hulton Archive / Stringer 64, Imagno 59, Keystone 97, 135r, Keystone / Stringer 50, 116, Keystone / Stringer 50, 116, New York Times Co. 7b, 135l, Roger Viollet Collection 89, ullstein bild 44, 81, 96, 111, 123, Universal History Archive 102, UniversalImagesGroup 132; **Bildarchiv Preussischer Kulturbesitz:** 28, 30, 35, 75, 112, 28, 30, 35, 75, 112; **Mary Evans Picture Library:** Sueddeutsche Zeitung Photo 108, 117, 120, 131; **Punch Cartoon Library:** 70; **SuperStock:** Past Pix / SSPL / Science and Society 46; **TopFoto:** 85, Ullsteinbild 55, 67

Cover images: *Front:* **Bridgeman Art Library Ltd:** Private Collection

All other images © Pearson Education

Every effort has been made to trace the copyright holders and we apologise in advance for any unintentional omissions. We would be pleased to insert the appropriate acknowledgement in any subsequent edition of this publication.

We are grateful to the following for permission to reproduce copyright material:

Text

Extract on page 9 in Source A from Selections from the Smuts Papers: *Volume IV November 1918-August 1919.* p.271 (Hancock W.K., and Van Der Poel, J.), CUP; Extract on page 9 in Interpretation 1 from *The Weimar Republic; Seminar Studies in History series,* 2nd ed., Longman (Hiden, J. 1996) 2, Taylor and Francis Group with permission; Extract in Source B on page 10 from *Rethinking the Weimar Republic - Authority and Authoritarianism 1916-1936,* Bloomsbury (McElligott,A 2014) 9, © Bloomsbury Academic, an imprint of Bloomsbury Publishing Plc.; Extract in Interpretation 2 on page 15 from *The Coming of the Third Reich,* Penguin (Evans, R.J. 2004), (Penguin Books 2003). Copyright © Richard Evans 2003.Used by permission of Penguin Press, an imprint of Penguin Publishing Group, a division of Penguin Random House LLC.; Extract on page 19 in Interpretation 1 *The Coming of the Third Reich,* Penguin (Evans, R.J. 2004), (Penguin Books 2003). Copyright © Richard Evans 2003.Used by permission of Penguin Press, an imprint of Penguin Publishing Group, a division of Penguin Random House LLC.; Extract on page 27 in Source A from *Stresemann and the Politics of the Weimar Republic,* Princeton University Press (Turner, H.A. 1963) p.164. Reproduced with permission of Princeton University Press in the format Book via Copyright Clearance Center; Extract on page 31 in Interpretation 1 from *Nationalism, Dictatorship and Democracy in the 20th Century Europe* (Hall,K.,Shuter,J.,Brown,D.,Williams,B. 2015) p.17, Pearson Education Limited ;Extract on page 33 in Interpretation 1 from HTA Modern History Study Guide (2nd Edition) Editor Paul Kiem 2007 Student resources published by Charles Sturt University, New South Wales, Australia., http://hsc.csu.edu.au/modern_history/national_studies/germany/2423/page127.htm, Courtesy NSW Department of Education. Reproduced with permission; Extract in Interpretation 2 on page 34 from Anticipating the Future in the Present: "New Women" and Other Beings of the Future in Weimar Germany, *Central European History* 42, pp.662-663 (Graf,R. 2009), © Conference Group for Central European History of the American Historical Association doi:10.1017/S0008938909991026, Cambridge University Press with permission; Extract on page 36 in Interpretation 3 from *Weimar and Nazi Germany: Heinemann Secondary History Project,* Heinemann (Lee, S. 1996); Extract on page 44 in Interpretation 1 from *Weimar and Nazi Germany,* Heinemann (Lee,S.) p.27, Pearson Education Limited; Extract on page 46 in Interpretation 3 from *The Weimar Republic,* Longman (Hiden, J. 1996) p.45, Taylor and Francis Group with permission; Extract on page 49 in Interpretation 1 from *The Coming of the Third Reich,* Penguin (Evans, R.J. 2004), (Penguin Books 2003). Copyright

© Richard Evans 2003.Used by permission of Penguin Press, an imprint of Penguin Publishing Group, a division of Penguin Random House LLC.; Extract on page 54 in Interpretation 3 from *The Coming of the Third Reich,* Penguin (Evans, R.J. 2004), (Penguin Books 2003). Copyright © Richard Evans 2003. Used by permission of Penguin Press, an imprint of Penguin Publishing Group, a division of Penguin Random House LLC; Extract on page 62 in Interpretation 1 from The Coming of the Third Reich, Penguin (Evans, R.J. 2004), (Penguin Books 2003). Copyright © Richard Evans 2003.Used by permission of Penguin Press, an imprint of Penguin Publishing Group, a division of Penguin Random House LLC; Extract on page 63 in Interpretation 2 from *The Weimar Republic,* Longman (Hiden, J. 1996) p.64, Taylor and Francis Group with permission; Extract on page 64 in Interpretation 3 from *Adolf Hitler,* Doubleday (Tolund,J 1976), Excerpt from ADOLF HITLER by John Toland, copyright © 1976 by John Toland. Used by permission of Doubleday, an imprint of the Knopf Doubleday Publishing Group, and a division of Penguin Random House LLC. All rights reserved. Extract on page 69 in Interpretation 1 from *The Coming of the Third Reich,* Penguin (Evans, R.J. 2004), (Penguin Books 2003). Copyright © Richard Evans 2003.Used by permission of Penguin Press, an imprint of Penguin Publishing Group, a division of Penguin Random House LLC; Extract on page 69 in Source C from Berlin Stories, Reissue ed., New Directions by Christopher Isherwood, copyright © Christopher Isherwood 1935, used by permission of The Wylie Agency (UK) Limited and by permission of New Directions Publishing Corp; Extract on page 77 in Source G from *The Nemesis of Power: The German Army in Politics 1918_1845,* Palgrave Macmillan (Sir John Wheeler-Bennet) reproduced with permission of Palgrave Macmillan; Extract on page 80 in Interpretation 1 from *Life in Germany c1919-c1945,* Pearson 2009 (Waugh, S.) Pearson Education Limited ; Extract on page 85 in Interpretation 2 from *The Nazis: A Warning from History,* BBC Books (Rees,L.), The Random House Group; Extract on page 95 in Interpretation 1 from Holocaust Encyclopedia, http://www.ushmm.org/wlc/en/article.php?ModuleId=10007519, Culture in the Third Reich: Disseminating the Nazi Worldview: United States Holocaust Memorial Museum, U.S.; Extract on page 100 in Source A from *Germany: The Third Reich,* Hodder and Stoughton (Layton, G. 1992) p.83, reproduced by permission of Hodder Education; Extract on page 101 in Interpretation 1 from *The Nazi Dictatorship: Problems and Perspectives of Interpretation,* Edward Arnold (Kershaw, I 1985) p.174, reproduced by permission of Hodder Education; Extract on page 103 in Source E from *Opposition and Resistance in Nazi Germany,* CUP (McDonough, F. 2001); Extract on page 111 in Source F from *Nazi Women,* New ed., Channel 4 books (Haste, C. 2003) p.91, Peters Fraser & Dunlop with permission; Extract on page 112 in Source H from *Nazi Women,* Channel 4 Books (Haste, C. 2001) p.96, Peters Fraser & Dunlop with permission; Extract on page 118 in Source E from *Nazi Culture: Intellectual, Cultural, and Social Life in the Third Reich,* University of Wisconsin Press (Mosse, G.L. 2003) p.277, Mosse, George L.Nazi Culture. © 2003 by the Board of Regents of the University of Wisconsin System. Reprinted by permission of The University of Wisconsin Press; Extract on page 118 in Source G from

A Hitler Youth: Growing Up in Germany in the 1930s, New Ed edition, The History Press Ltd (Metelmann,H.) with permission from The History Press; Extract on page 118 in Interpretation 1 from *Modern Germany,* Cambridge University Press (Berghahn, V.R. 1982) p.134; Extract on page 121 in Source M from *Inside Nazi Germany,* Batsford (Peukert, D. 1987) Yale University Press and Peukert, Detler J.K., Inside Nazi Germany (1987). Reproduced with kind permission of B.T. Batsford, part of Pavilion Books Company Limited; Extract on page 129 in Interpretation 3 from *Life in Germany,* Pearson (Waugh, S. 2009) p.85, Pearson Education Limited; Extract on page 129 in Interpretation 4 from *Nationalism, dictatorship and democracy in 20th Century Europe,* Pearson (Hall, Shuter, Brown, Williams 2015) p.77, Pearson Education Limited; Article on page 136 in Source G from *Daily Telegraph,* November 1938, Telegraph Media Group Ltd 2016; Extract on page 153 in Interpretation 1 from *Weimar and Nazi Germany,* Heinemann (Lee, S 1996), Pearson Education Limited; Extract on page 153 in Interpretation 2 from *GCSE Modern World History for Edexcel: Nazi Germany 1930-39,* Hodder Murray (Waugh, S. and Wright, J. 2007), reproduced by permission of Hodder Education.